A Color Handbook of
BIOLOGICAL CONTROL IN PLANT PROTECTION

- **Neil Helyer**
  HNC, MBPR (Hort)
  Fargro Ltd, Littlehampton, UK

- **Kevin Brown**
  BSc, DPhil
  Ecotox Ltd, Tavistock, Devon, UK

- **Nigel D Cattlin**
  Holt Studios, UK

TIMBER PRESS
PORTLAND, OREGON

Published in North America in 2003 by
Timber Press, Inc.
The Haseltine Building
133 S. W. Second Avenue, Suite 450
Portland, Oregon 97204, USA

ISBN 0-88192-599-3

A CIP record for this book is available from the Library of Congress.

Commissioning editor: Jill Northcott
Project manager: Paul Bennett
Copy-editor: Ruth C Maxwell
Designer: Cathy Martin, Presspack Computing
Cover designer: Patrick Daly
Color reproduction: Acumen Colour Ltd
Printed in Spain

Contents

Preface

Despite great current interest in the subject, and its importance to growers and scientists alike, books on biological pest control are still uncommon and mostly unsatisfactory (we have referenced the best of these). Several make passing reference to a few common beneficial organisms, but most are concerned with the pest species and the plant damage they cause. In this brief volume we have tried to go some way towards rectifying this situation. Developing from an idea expressed to us by Dr Paul Jepson, now at Oregon State University, the aim has been to produce a handbook containing profiles and colour photographs of as many examples of biological control organisms representative of as wide a global area as possible.

Each profile is divided into four sections: species characteristics, including organism size, host food and closely related species; life cycle; crop/pest associations; and influences on growing practices. The section on crop/pest associations describes how and when the organism attacks its prey, the crops and environments in which it is likely to be found, and whether it is com-

mercially available. The section on the influence on growing practices completes each profile by summarizing how growers can make best use of these natural enemies, and often makes mention of harmful, safe and IPM-compatible pesticides.

Although all the organisms occur naturally in various parts of the world and several are commercially mass-produced, many can only be found in their natural environment and usually close to their food sources. We therefore thought that a short section on the pests was essential, since all the natural enemies require a host for their survival.

We hope this handbook will be useful to advisers, extension officers, educators and research workers, and to all growers with an eye for the environment, no matter how large or small the area under production.

Neil Helyer
Kevin Brown
Nigel Cattlin

Acknowledgements

For providing technical information and organisms to photograph:

Becker Underwood, Littlehampton, UK

Jude Bennison, ADAS, Boxworth, Cambridgeshire, UK

Dr. John Buxton, ADAS Rosemaunde, Herefordshire, UK

Dr. Dave Chandler, Horticulture Research International, Wellesbourne, UK

Dr. Michael de Courcy Williams, Horticulture Research International, Wellesbourne, UK

Dr. David R. Gillespie, Section Head, IPM and Research Scientist. Agriculture and Agri-Food, Canada

Dr. Richard GreatRex, Syngenta Bioline, Little Clacton, Essex, UK

Dr Paul Jarrett, Horticulture Research International, Wellesbourne, UK

Professor Paul Jepson, Dept of Entomology, Oregon State University, USA.

Dr Garry Keane, Horticulture Research International, Wellesbourne, UK

Mike Mead-Briggs, Mambo-Tox Ltd, Southampton, UK

Dr. Graeme Murphy, Ontario Ministry of Agriculture and Food, Vineland, Ontario, Canada

Dr. Marilyn Steiner, National Centre for Greenhouse Horticulture, New South Wales Agriculture, Gosford, Australia

Les Wardlow, L.R. Wardlow, Ashford, Kent, UK

SECTION 1:
CROP ENVIRONMENTS

- ARABLE CROPS
- FRUIT PRODUCTION
- PROTECTED CROP SYSTEMS

Pests and their associated natural enemies occur on most plants whether grown as arable crops (**1–7**) on cultivated land, as semi-permanent crops (soft fruit and orchards), or those protected within a structure. These growing systems occur at various scales of size, from extremely large areas of broad acre mono-culture arable crops to small areas such as glasshouses and private gardens. The larger scale crops tend to receive lower levels of input and can thus be regarded as loosely managed in terms of man hours per given area. Fruit production (**8–14**) is generally on a smaller scale and is more closely managed, while protected crop systems (**15–21**) are intensively managed throughout much of the cropping cycle. The three crop environments discussed in this chapter cover the main growing systems world-wide, but are equally relevant regardless of the size of enterprise. So a mixed cropping, large private garden with a small glasshouse, vegetable plot, soft fruit and top (tree) fruit can have the same pest spectrum as the largest farm, orchard or protected nursery. However, with a greater variety of plants there inevitably comes a wider range of pests and (hopefully) their natural enemies. Apart from climatic variations the crop/pest associations will be similar for the various plants grown in each location. For example, many cereal pests occur only on cereals or grasses and are unable to survive on other plants, while pests on protected crops grown in cool temperate regions may be found outside in the tropics and warm temperate climates.

Arable Crops

ARABLE CROPS (1–4)

Plants produced in open field, cultivated land (including minimum tillage) with an annual harvest are regarded as arable crops. They include cereals, field beans, peas, potatoes, beet and oil seed crops. However, ecologically the most interesting is the increasing area of 'set-aside' arable land, which includes thousands of hectares under 'game cover' and hundreds of thousands of hectares under 'natural regeneration'. These areas are not sprayed with pesticides and have a wider range of host plants, which support a more diverse fauna. The steady expansion in organic farming has also led to a more positive approach to the management of local biodiversity for its own sake and also to encourage the contribution of natural enemies to the protection of organic crops.

THE ENVIRONMENT

The optimum environment for beneficial insects would be one where there was sufficient suitable prey to fuel their reproduction, minimal use of harmful pesticides and suitable over-wintering sites within striking distance of the host plants, to ensure their continued survival.

From both an ecological and economic point of view, arable crops differ from orchards and protected crops in several important aspects as far as their value as a haven for beneficial insects is concerned. Arable crops have considerably lower gross margins than protected crops and even orchard crops, so the costs of inputs are severely restricted. This is the most important influence on the management of beneficial insects in arable crops and why the approach to Integrated Pest Management (IPM) in arable crops is so different to that in high value horticultural crops.

EXTENSIVE PRODUCTION SITES

Arable crops are grown extensively over millions of hectares, often with fewer windbreaks or hedgerows than orchard crops and certainly without the luxury of heated glasshouses to provide protection for beneficial insects from winter conditions. This will have an impact on the speed at which beneficial insects will recolonize large fields in the spring, as distances from their over-wintering sites increase. Many beneficial species, particularly carabid beetles (Péter *et al.*, 2001), over-winter in the soil beneath hedgerows. If

1 A young potato crop.

2 Poppies flowering in an unsprayed barley field margin.

beneficial insects are slow to distribute within a crop, pest numbers can increase in their absence and growers are more likely to apply a pesticide as a routine measure to protect their crops from pest damage. Pests such as aphids can arrive suddenly in large numbers and if growers also consider them a risk as virus vectors for barley yellow dwarf virus, the pressure to spray agrochemicals to control them increases.

LOWER BUDGETS FOR CROP PROTECTION INPUTS

IPM in protected crops is well developed and relies on the introduction of commercially raised beneficial insects and their integration with compatible pesticides. Beneficial insects are expensive and establishing them in a crop relies on close crop monitoring, to ensure that sufficient prey are present to guarantee that a single introduction will establish. Another approach is to make several consecutive introductions of beneficial insects to overcome the problem of insufficient prey at the time of introduction. Detailed, skilled crop monitoring of this sort can also be an expensive input, outside the range of most arable crop budgets.

Pesticides which are compatible with beneficial insects tend to be very specific in the target pest or disease which they control and for this reason have a more limited market. The laws of supply and demand dictate that they are therefore often much more expensive than the broad-spectrum pesticides which can be sold into a wider market and are therefore cheaper. Consequently, the introduction of commercially raised beneficial insects to arable crops and the regular use of compatible pesticides, as well as the management time required to monitor the predator–prey relationships, is well out of the crop protection budget of most arable crops.

As in many countries, data are collected from farmers and growers in the UK to produce statistical tables relating to crop production. In the UK, the Department of Environment, Food and Rural Affairs (DEFRA, formerly Ministry of Agriculture, Fisheries and Food [MAFF]) publishes such surveys every 4–6 years (Garthwaite, et al., 1998) and routinely indicate that fungicides are the most extensively used pesticides on most British arable crops. Where an insecticide is applied it is usually a pyrethroid, such as cypermethrin, for the control of aphids. Pyrethroids are the cheapest group of agrochemicals and are therefore generally the most widely used on arable crops. They have a short harvest interval, so crops can be harvested almost immediately after application without harm to the consumer.

However, pyrethroids are harmful to most beneficial insects and are likely to kill more than 75% of any beneficial insects that they come into contact with at the time of spraying. More importantly, this harmful effect on beneficial insects is likely to last on the sprayed leaf for up to 12 weeks after the day of application. Unfortunately, pyrethroids do not have such a persistent harmful effect on the pests and may need to be sprayed more than once. This will prevent the migration of beneficial insects into the sprayed area and delay their impact as biological control agents for the target pest.

EFFECT OF TIMING OF PESTICIDE APPLICATIONS TO CEREALS ON BENEFICIAL INSECTS

For many years regulatory authorities have monitored and funded various research projects to determine the environmental impact of pesticide usage in arable crops. The Boxworth Project in the 1980s (Greig-Smith, 1991) examined the effects of intensive pesticide use in winter wheat on populations of small mammals, birds, invertebrates and plants in southern England. Monitoring over five years indicated that insects and spiders were particularly vulnerable to pesticide usage, and some species of carabids (ground beetles) and springtails disappeared.

It has been estimated that most of the 25,000 species of terrestrial arthropods in the UK exist in farmland (Aldridge and Carter, 1992), and over 99% of these are either natural enemies of crop pests, pollinators or food items of other farmland fauna (Brown, 1989).

Autumn-sown cereals are likely to be sprayed with a pyrethroid for the control of aphids in the autumn. The non-target fauna, which could be exposed to pesticides at this time, are the autumn- and winter-active carabids (*Bembidion obtusum*, *Nebria brevicollis*, *Notiophilius biguttatus* and *Trechus quadristriatus*) and staphylinids, springtails, mites, lycosid and linyphiid spiders (Cilgi and Vickerman, 1994). Ironically, carabids, staphylinids and spiders are important predators of aphids, the target pest of the sprays that are applied. Carabids are also very susceptible to chemical slug controls such as methiocarb. Again, carabids are natural enemies of slugs and while the use of slug pellets protects plants from slug damage, they also kill the natural enemies of slugs.

3 A tractor-mounted sprayer treating a wheat crop.

4 Sunflowers in Tuscany.

Studies have shown, however, that spiders, staphylinids and carabids are able to recover from autumn/winter applied pesticides, by the following summer (Vickerman, 1992). However, further applications of pyrethroids in the summer would prevent this resurgence.

In an unmanaged natural ecosystem, the natural enemy populations usually build up after the peak in the prey (pest) population. This delay can allow some pest damage to occur at the beginning of the season. The delicate balancing act which the grower faces is to decide whether this damage is economically significant enough to warrant spraying or whether it is safe to delay spraying and allow the beneficial insects to build up and control the pest. However, if the natural enemies are not present in sufficient numbers relative to the pest to prevent economic damage, the grower may consider their presence irrelevant in the crop protection scheme and spray.

MONITORING LEVELS OF BENEFICIAL INSECTS IN ARABLE FIELDS (5–7)

In order to assess the potential contribution of natural enemies they must first be captured and identified. Choosing the appropriate sampling method and the time of year and time of day when the sampling is conducted relies on knowledge of the life cycle and behaviour of the natural enemy in question.

CARABID BEETLES

The ecology of carabids has been studied extensively (Luff, 1987), and there is sufficient information about the life cycles of the most abundant species to determine when and how to capture them. For example, some carabids such as *Agonum dorsale* and *Bembidion lampros* are characteristically ground-active, which means that they can be caught in pit-fall traps placed in the soil. These consist of a container without a lid or lip which is sunk into the ground so that the mouth is level with the soil. The open mouth should be protected to exclude rain and other large animals such as toads from falling in, without preventing insects from entering. Preferably the ground should fall away from the mouth of the container to reduce the risk of flooding. Traps should be examined daily or contain a liquid preservative (e.g. 50% ethanediol), since many carabids are cannibalistic.

Window traps are used to monitor the movement of flying carabids and consist of vertical pieces of clear rigid Perspex, supported at various heights above the ground. These obstruct the flight of beetles, which collide into it and fall into a trough of preserving fluid below the window. They should be placed strategically in natural flight paths, such as between trees or in an opening between trees. Alternatively, sweep nets that consist of strong metal hoops about 40 cm in diameter with a 30 cm handle and a calico collection bag fixed to the hoop, can be used to collect beetles in the canopy. The net is swept to and fro in front of the collector whilst walking through the crop or area to be monitored. For more information refer to Forsythe (1987).

Demetrias atricapillus climbs up into cereal ears and the upper leaves and is more likely to be caught in a sweep net or suction sampling with a bug-vacuum than a pitfall trap. The larvae and adults of *D. atricapillus* are mostly nocturnal. Hence the activity of the natural enemy should be known in order that samples are taken at the appropriate time of day for a nocturnal or diurnal beetle. Suction sampling and sweep nets will also collect other flying natural enemies of aphids such as lacewing, hoverflies and parasitoid wasps.

STAPHYLINID BEETLES

Staphylinid beetles can be predators, parasitoids, fungivores or detritivores and can occur in very high numbers in arable crop systems. While the ecology of some species is known there are many for which little information is available. The smaller staphylinids can be quite difficult to identify and they have often been overlooked or lumped together at the sub-family level in agricultural field studies. Like carabid beetles staphylinids are easy to sample in arable systems using pitfall traps. Certain staphylinind species, e.g. *Tachinus signatus* and *Stenus clavicornis*, appear to be particularly susceptible to pyrethroid insecticides. While pitfall traps are a useful and cost effective way of determining the beneficial arthropod fauna of particular fields, it is worth noting that they only sample mobile species and that catch size is strongly affected by the weather conditions.

5 A D-vac sampler used to collect small arthropods, in this case in a ripe wheat field.

6 A pitfall trap used to sample ground-active arthropods in arable crops.

LINYPHIID SPIDERS

Spiders are one of the most important predatory groups in arable ecosystems (Nyfeller and Benz, 1987). Despite their potential to support a rich spider fauna, individual fields have been found to show considerable variation in the numbers of individuals and species present. Toft (1989) showed that in some fields spiders were as abundant as in natural habitats, whereas in the USA Nyfeller *et al.* (1994) reported sparse spider populations from agricultural fields. Samu *et al.* (2001) found that spider assemblages of Hungarian cereal fields were dominated by five species (*Pardosa agrestis*, *Meineta rurestris*, *Oedothorax apicatus*, *Pachygnatha degeeri* and *Tibellus oblongus*). These dominant species were found in every field sampled in different regions of Hungary.

While the exact species composition may differ between countries a similar pattern has been observed throughout Europe (Luczak, 1975). The most common linyphiid spiders found in arable crops in northern Europe include *Erigone atra*, *E. dentipalpis*, *Lepthyphantes tenuis*, *Bathyphantes gracilis*, *Meioneta rurestris* and *Oedothorax fuscus* (Sunderland *et al.*, 1986; Topping and Sunderland, 1992). Their sampling and identification are relatively easy (Everts *et al.*, 1989) and they can be extracted from crops by the use of a portable 'suction sampler' which sucks them from the canopy into a collection bag, as well as by using pitfall traps. Linyphiid spiders are often caught in large numbers in arable crops in the autumn and winter (Sunderland *et al.*, 1986). Some of these spiders can also be reared in the laboratory (Everts *et al.*, 1989), which opens up the possibility of augmenting field populations if 'low-tech' farm rearing methods are developed. Spiders have a high dispersal ability, which makes them a valuable natural enemy in the large fields which are characteristic of arable systems.

INTEGRATED CROP MANAGEMENT (ICM)

There are now strong political pressures in the European Union to reduce inputs in arable crops, which has led to the development and evaluation of less intensive and ecologically more sustainable crop husbandry methods. The success of such systems however, needs not only to be measured in the increase of biodiversity but in the continued profitability of the farm. Farming in general is under increasing financial pressure as a result of falling profitability. Not only are more farmers leaving the industry, but also agricultural colleges are finding it hard to recruit new entrants into agriculture. Farmers are the countryside stewards and without their management the value of land as a resource for the production of food would diminish, as would access as farmland reverted to scrub.

The future of farming lies in maintaining profitability. This might be achieved by distinguishing their products as having being produced under a more environmentally sound system, such as ICM or organic production. These systems integrate chemical, biological, cultural and physical controls to reduce crop protection inputs.

Recognizing the potential value in the market place of such systems, research into integrated production methods in Europe has made rapid progress in recent years. Several research projects aimed at developing on-farm alternatives and management skills which will maintain species diversity (amongst other things) while sustaining farm incomes (Jordan, 1998) are well underway. Farmers and growers are able to have their environmental farm policy and pest control strategies accredited by independent audit. In many instances this is part of the marketing requirement to enable producers to supply directly to the large multiple retail outlets (supermarkets).

Farmers and growers are able to have their environmental farm policy accredited by independent audit; in the UK audit is performed through the auspices of Linking Environment and Farming. This organization provides technical assistance, through close association with the Farming and Wildlife Advisory Group, to develop wildlife conservation plans on farms and accredit the environmentally sensitive farming methods employed. In support of these developments, the Countryside Stewardship Scheme offers payments to farmers that further encourages conservation plans as part of the land management programme on a farm.

CONSERVATION HEADLANDS AND BEETLE BANKS

Conservation strategies are a less expensive means of encouraging natural enemies into a crop, where low gross margins inhibit the inundative release of commercially raised beneficial insects. Research and development of conservation headlands has shown the benefits of a 6 m-wide strip between the crop edge and first tramline that is treated with selective pesticides to control certain weeds while allowing broad-leaved weeds and beneficial organisms to survive. Beetle banks are grass ridges, which can be positioned in the middle of large fields to form refuges for spiders, staphylinid and carabid beetles. This enables predators to over-winter more effectively in mid field refuges from where they can spread into the crop in the spring.

While crop protection is just one aspect of crop production, both ICM and organic systems require a better understanding of the role of beneficial organisms and skills in their identification in order to reduce reliance on pesticides. Recognizing the difference between a pest and a beneficial is just the first step to a more sustainable farming future.

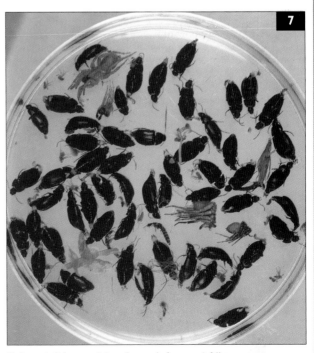

7 A petri dish containing the catch from a pitfall trap.

Fruit Production

INTRODUCTION (8–14)

Despite such a broad heading the natural enemies of fruit crops are surprisingly similar, irrespective of whether the crop is strawberries or cranberries in the USA or is apples or pears in Europe. The same predators and parasitoids feature as antagonists of aphids and mites, scale insects and leaf rollers (tortrix moth larvae) in almost all crop systems. Indeed, the same pest species also feature in different crops and different continents. Although there are often geographical differences as to which are the relevant species it is usually the same genus and the same type of organisms which attack key pest species. For this reason many of the species descriptions given in this book are equally applicable to North America and to northern and southern Europe.

Fruit crops can range in size from a hundred or so plants or trees in a small plot to many hectares of continuous culture. Tree crops can contain mature individually spaced trees, lines of espalier trained trees or comprise multi-row blocks of small trees. The ground under the plants may be bare earth, neatly mown grass or mixed vegetation. The margins and boundaries may be old diverse hedgerows, coniferous windbreak trees or simply a barbed wire fence. With such a range of possibilities it is difficult to generalize about fruit crops. While many pest species will be attracted to orchards irrespective of their configuration, their natural enemies may be more discerning. Immaculate rows of small trees with bare earth beneath them will present few hiding places and little alternative food for voracious predators. That does not mean that weed-free crops are inherently unsuitable for beneficial arthropods. However, if pest numbers fall within the crop then the predators may leave altogether rather than move to nearby food on other plants.

Unlike the glasshouse environment, where predators and parasitoids can be bought and released to target specific pests, fruit crops are unconfined and open to the elements. It is not usually practical to buy and release beneficial arthropods. Extremely large numbers would be needed and they would be unlikely to be seen again. The key to establishing biological control in commercial fruit crops is to encourage and enhance populations of the naturally occurring predators and parasitoids.

Predators in fruit crops fall into two distinct types, residents and colonists. The resident species are present throughout the whole of a growing season and are established and well placed to feed on the early pest individuals as they arrive in an orchard. Residents tend to be polyphagous and will occur whether or not there is an apparent source of prey. Two important residents in fruit orchards are often earwigs and spiders. Although earwigs may be considered to be a pest since they can damage the surface of the fruit, particularly in crops such as peaches and apricots, they are also predators of aphids and mites and can occur in very high numbers in orchards. Since they are active at night and hidden in crevices during the day, earwigs are often overlooked.

The colonists include predatory bugs of the families Anthocoridae, Miridae and Nabidae together with coccinellid beetles, hoverflies and lacewings. Colonists tend to be attracted to an orchard because of the presence of prey (usually in the form of a pest outbreak). Since colonists are usually highly mobile they can occur in extremely high numbers. For some colonists such as hoverflies and some lacewings, only the larval life stage is predatory, whereas for others, such as predatory bugs and ladybirds like *Coccinella septempunctata*, both the larvae and the adults are predatory.

Fruit crops can be managed so as to nurture field resident populations of natural enemies and to provide an environment where immigrant predators and parasitoids can become established and thrive.

PESTICIDE USE AND NATURAL ENEMIES

Not surprisingly the first step to enhancing naturally occurring biological control agents is to examine carefully the use of pesticides, particularly insecticides and acaricides. In the winter months applications of broad-spectrum products such as pyrethroids and organophosphates may not be damaging to beneficial populations. The majority will be

8 A flowering orchard with untreated undergrowth.

9 Ripening clementines in a Spanish citrus orchard.

hidden away in crevices or present as eggs and relatively protected in the bark of trees. Broad-spectrum pesticides can have a place in an IPM programme if they are used at the right time of year. For a grower to determine the likely risk to non-target arthropods from a product he should consult the label and seek confirmation either from the literature, web-sites or an advisor as to the likely impact. For many years the members of the IOBC/WPRS working group on Pesticides and Beneficial Organisms screened new and existing products for harmlessness using 'worst case' laboratory tests. Their findings (e.g. Hassan *et al.*, 1983, 1987) were published in terms of a classification from 1 to 4 (1 being harmless and 4 being harmful). While these results are useful they must be treated with some caution. Products found to be harmless can be considered to be of low risk in the field, whereas those found to be harmful in these tests require further evaluation to determine the magnitude and duration of any effects that would occur in a crop system.

Although the majority of fungicides are considered to be relatively harmless to insects and mites, most organo-phosphate products, whatever their intended use, are insecti-cidal and can be very harmful to predators and parasitoids. Sulphur, commonly applied as a fungicide in France, is particularly damaging to populations of predatory mites such as *Typhlodromus pyri* and *Amblyseius (Neoseiulus) californicus*. Since these are relatively immobile mites that can be important predators of spider mites, their presence is desirable. Very often the first signs a grower will notice when he has killed predatory mites with a broad-spectrum product will be an outbreak of spider mites that were previously being controlled. Fungicides containing the active ingredient mancozeb are not harmful to predatory mites after the first application but typically affect them adversely after a fourth or fifth treatment in a single season. Amongst the acaricides there are a number of products which are relatively selective, e.g. the growth regulators, which tend to be more effective against spider mites than against predatory mites, and some of which only have a limited effect against the beneficial taxa. Growth regulators do not give immediate control (often working only when the pest would have moulted) and for this reason have sometimes been avoided by growers looking for a quick kill with a dramatic knockdown.

Where aphids are a problem the use of selective aphicides can result in minimal disturbance of non-target insects. When broad-spectrum insecticides are used to control a particular pest problem it is usually preferable to select a product which is relatively short lived. Products such as chlorpyrifos are highly efficacious insecticides and will certainly kill most pest and beneficial mites, spiders and insects in a treated crop. However, they will undergo relatively rapid chemical degradation and the leaves and fruit will no longer be toxic to immigrant predators and parasitoids after about ten days. Of course larger orchards will be less readily colonized than smaller ones.

Intelligent selection of pesticides is a critical component to optimize the role of natural enemies in pest control. While it is relatively easy to recommend using a small number of relatively selective molecules it is very dangerous for IPM to become totally dependent on them. For several years IPM in a range of fruit crops in southern Europe relied heavily on treatments with the growth regulator diflubenzuron and with phosalone, together with the actions of beneficial arthropods. Just when the growers were congratulating themselves on the continued success of their IPM programmes the major pests became resistant to these two products. Faced with uncontrollable pests the growers resorted to broad-spectrum products. While they were aware of the value and importance of their natural enemies it was more important for them to safeguard their crops.

Unfortunately for the growers the pests had also developed cross-resistance to many products, particularly in populations of the codling moth, *Cydia pomonella*. In parts of southern France the codling moth is now unaffected by many insecticides and resistance is a serious problem. At the time of writing only azinphos-methyl and flufenoxuron (an insect growth regulator [IGR] which is relatively difficult for insects to metabolize) give effective control. However, repeated applications of products like azinphos-methyl have devastated populations of virtually all the main biological control agents. Interestingly, some predators in a few localities have also been found to be resistant to organo-phosphates. The key point to arise from this is that IPM strategies should not rely heavily on only one or two types of chemistry for their pest control.

The use of smart methods of control, which affect only the pest species, such as mating disruption techniques and attract and lure baits with pheromones, are preferable to spraying and these are becoming more widely used. Careful choice of crop protection products is critical to maintaining biodiversity

10 A tractor and air-assisted sprayer treating an apple orchard.

11 Honey bee, a beneficial insect, on an apple blossom.

within fruit crops. The recent IOBC/WPRS guidelines for integrated production of pome fruits in Europe (Cross, 2002) state nine criteria that should be taken into account when considering the suitability of products for use. These are its toxicity to man, toxicity to key natural enemies, toxicity to other natural organisms, pollution of ground and surface water, ability to stimulate pests, selectivity, persistence, incomplete information and the necessity for use. Based on these criteria the IOBC/WPRS sub-group for integrated fruit production consider pyrethroid insecticides and acaricides, non-naturally occurring plant growth regulators, organochlorine insecticides and acaricides and toxic, water polluting or very persistent herbicides to be incompatible with integrated fruit production.

The fruit crop habitat itself can be enhanced to encourage predators and parasitoids. Early in the season, before any pest species have been observed on the fruit trees, quite large numbers of predators, particularly Heteroptera such as *Orius* or *Deraeocoris* spp., have been observed on weed species in the margins or in the under-storey of orchards which are not being intensively managed. As the season progresses these species are found on the trees themselves, feeding on spider mites, aphids and psyllids. Such predators often over-winter beneath bark or in dead leaves and appear to favour a sheltered protected environment from which to extend their activity up into the trees. The provision of areas of 'weeds' in the margins of orchards or allowing a mixture of plant species to grow underneath the fruit trees will definitely encourage predators. If pesticides are applied to an orchard then the under-storey vegetation or refugia will provide shelter and perhaps unsprayed reservoirs from which predators can recolonize trees. Addition of flowering plants both within orchards and at their margins has been shown to increase predator abundance, particularly of spiders.

However, when these plants are flowering care must be taken to avoid spraying any pesticides which would be toxic to honeybees or bumble bees. Functional bio-diversity is the current term for allowing a wider range of plants and associated insects to flourish within fruit crops. It is impractical for growers to identify all the plant and invertebrates within the crop so attention is now focusing on identification of one or more bio-indicator (Brown, 2001) or bio-marker guilds. These guilds are made up of species known to react to impacts or change within the ecosystem (Paoletti and Bressan, 1996). Concern over 'bio-indicator' terminology and its meaning is discussed by van Gestel and van Brummelen (1996). Bio-indicators will allow managers to determine the health of a system without needing to survey and identify all the invertebrates.

An additional step is to provide a source of prey early in the growing season, for example by introducing plant species which are attacked by their own aphids or mites particularly early in the year. As long as the plants are carefully selected their aphids will be specific and will not feed on the fruit trees. However, many of the aphid predators such as hoverflies, coccinellids and lacewings may be attracted into to the orchard by the aphids on the so called weeds but will feed equally well on the aphids on the trees. If flowering plants are also present in the orchard then these will provide a source of pollen (which can serve as a secondary food for predatory mites and predatory bugs such as *Anthocoris* spp.) and will attract hoverflies, the larvae of which are predators of aphids.

As well as the area of the crop itself the margins and boundaries can be managed to make them attractive to beneficial species, e.g. by planting appropriate tree species for

12 Codling moth (*Cydia pomonella*) exit hole in a ripe apple.

13 Sheets beneath apple trees used to collect an insect population.

14 Raspberry fruit.

oviposition by predatory bugs. The neighbouring crops and habitats will also strongly affect the overall abundance of predatory and parasitoid species in a given location. Boller (2001) gives examples from Swiss vineyards where protection of hedges and borders in close proximity to the crop is encouraged and where blackberries (*Rubus fruticosus*) provide a source of predatory phytoseiid mites (Baur *et al.*, 1998) and wild roses (*Rosa canina*) provide a source of host insects for the leafhopper parasitoid *Anagrus atomus*. Stinging nettles (*Urtica dioica*) are tolerated since they are a food plant for indifferent Lepidoptera and are important for building up their parasitoid complex.

Orchards backing onto woodland, grassland or simply other orchards which are rich in insects, spiders and mites will be likely to have colonists waiting in the wings to move in and begin feeding on pests. Unfortunately, the recent subsidy paid to growers to remove apple orchards in Europe resulted in destruction of many of the old and relatively unintensive orchards which harboured particularly high populations of virtually all of the beneficial groups. In part of the Ardeche region of France, apples and pears are grown in a patchwork of small orchards often with vines in adjacent blocks. The fruit is managed so as to encourage predators which can move freely from one orchard to another. Care is taken when treating the vines so not to over-spray the orchards.

The sex pheromones of many lepidopteran pests of fruit crops, including soft fruits, have been identified. However, relatively few non-lepidopteran pheromones have been isolated. Providing that it is economically viable such chemicals could be useful in sampling to determine timing of pesticide application or used in lure and kill baits as an alternative to spraying large areas of crop. Cross *et al.* (2000) describe developments in discovering the sex pheromones for three important pests of soft fruit, the European tarnished bug (*Lygus rugulipennis*), strawberry blossom weevil (*Anthnomus rubi*) and the blackcurrant leaf midge (*Dasineura tetensi*).

MAJOR PESTS

In the 1980s spider mites and aphids were probably the major pests in fruit orchards in Europe with psyllids, scales, codling moth and leaf rollers occurring as minor pests. In low input orchards in southern Europe it was not uncommon to see major outbreaks of fruit tree red spider mite which in turn attracted very high densities of predators such as the ladybird beetle *Stethorus punctillum*. Aphids, such as the woolly apple aphid, *Eriosoma lanigerum* would appear in large white waxy colonies and attract high numbers of the species specific parasitoid *Aphelinus mali*.

In recent years spider mites and aphids appear to have declined in importance and the codling moth and leaf rollers have increased to become the major pest species. Aphids and mites are external feeders on leaves and shoots of the trees and are readily accessible to predators and parasitoids. In contrast the larvae of codling moth quickly penetrate the apple or pear fruit and are protected from predation by the fruit itself. Biological control of codling moth using egg parasitoids, such as the tiny wasp *Trichogramma* spp. should be possible but to date has not been undertaken successfully. The parasitism rate would need to be extremely high to give good enough control. Growers cannot sell fruit with the blemish of an entry hole and would strive for very high levels of control. For this reason, chemical control has been the main method employed against codling moth. Since the period of egg laying and egg hatch may last for three or more

weeks it is often necessary to make three to four applications against the spring generation. The use of products which cause mating disruption of the moths has been increasing in importance and is harmless to other arthropod species.

A COMBINED APPROACH TO LIMITING PEST SPECIES

Growers often believe that the actions of one or two key species are responsible for all biological pest control in a commercial orchard. Classical examples of biological control tend to reinforce this hypothesis with well-known cases of one antagonist against one predator. In commercial orchards different predatory or parasitoid species tend to become the main antagonists in different growing seasons. Sometimes this is attributable to weather conditions or to the availability of suitable prey which will favour one particular species over another.

Looking at populations of pests, predators and parasitoids in fruit crops it seems that it is the combined efforts of all the beneficial arthropods which may actually limit or contain pest outbreaks. Mites, aphids and psyllids can be attacked by a diverse range of different predators and parasitoids, some of them generalists and some of them specific antagonists of individual pest species. At any time a single tree will contain a mixture of beneficial arthropod species depending on the time of year and the abundance of prey. For example, trees in a low input pear orchard in Provence, France sampled in May 1996 contained on average 250 predators and parasitoids per tree. Of these there were about 100 predatory bugs, 65 earwigs, 25 spiders, 17 ladybird beetles, 16 parasitic wasps, 10 lacewings, 8 hoverflies and 9 representatives of other predatory groups. This orchard had a small outbreak of pear Psylla which was clearly the primary food for the dominant bug species. The species composition and the relative abundance of different beneficial groups will differ between orchards in the same region in the same season and will also vary considerably between years.

In all field crops, and in fruit crops in particular, there is no one super-predator. The species which are bred and sold commercially tend to become well known and these usually represent the most important predatory and parasitoid groups. However, it is sometimes the lesser known insects such as the odd looking bug *Heterotoma planicornis* or perhaps action of unfashionable but purely predatory groups such as spiders which end up limiting pest populations in a particular orchard.

Protected Crop Systems

ACHIEVING EQUILIBRIUM (15–21)

Protected environments of the glasshouse, conservatory or similar structure limit the deleterious effects of the outside elements to enhance plant growth. In doing so, plants grow faster, bigger and better; consequently any pest or disease will have a favoured environment in which to do the maximum damage in the shortest possible time. Pests which naturally occur only during summer months may remain active throughout most of the year, e.g. summer tortrix moth in a heated structure will breed continuously. In unheated structures pests may not be active during the winter months but they will become evident much earlier in the growing season. During the early part of the growing season the protective structure not only reduces the effects of adverse weather conditions but can also prevent many natural enemies of pests from entering. This can work in the growers' favour: by introducing beneficial organisms early they are less likely to escape and more likely to control the pest infestations.

Once equilibrium has been achieved between pest and natural enemies the control programme becomes more stable. The idea of 'seeding' plants with a pest and later beneficial insects to create a bank of biological control agents was widely adopted in the early 1970s and is known as the 'classical' introduction method or 'banker plant system' (Hussey *et al.*, 1969). A modern variation on this theme is to use pests that are specific to a group of plants but which can sustain natural enemies capable of living off other pests. Trays of barley, wheat or pots of maize infested with cereal aphids are treated with parasitoids or predators (*Aphidius* or *Aphidoletes* spp.). When equilibrium has been achieved the plants are brought into the glasshouse where the parasitoids disperse to find other aphids to attack. The cereal aphids, being host plant specific are unable to survive on the main crop and pose no threat. This system works well in early planted cucumber crops where the principal aphid is *Aphis gossypii* which happens to have an extremely high rate of reproduction. The alternative host banker system continues to produce useful numbers of natural enemies for several weeks; usually long enough for good establishment of parasitoids or predators through the crop.

CROP MONITORING AND PEST CONTROL

Monocrop situations are the most vulnerable to attack: what could be better for a pest to establish and run havoc through than thousands of identical plants growing together, under ideal conditions? Mixed crop plantings generally have fewer overall problems but can suffer from 'hot spots' of trouble. In both situations prompt action can prevent a lot of damage being done. Crop monitoring by visual assessment of leaves and plants is the most accurate method of detecting a pest organism. However, coloured sticky traps are routinely used to monitor flying pests (Sunderland *et al.*, 1992). Yellow traps are for aphid, leaf miner, thrips and whitefly, blue are more selective, generally attracting sciarid fly and thrips, while orange are used for carrot fly. The addition of a sex attractant pheromone makes them even more effective. Sticky traps placed at the top of a crop will help reduce the pest population quite rapidly; in a small greenhouse they may suffice for the whole season.

Several natural enemies are available to use. Most are commercially mass-reared from individuals collected within the country of use, thus they are indigenous and require little or no registration for release. Many beneficial insects are host specific; aphid parasitoids have a limited host range, usually within a range of similar sized aphids, independent of the

15 Ripe strawberries in a modern commercial glasshouse.

16 Commercial polythene houses in Andalusia, southern Spain.

host plant. Predators tend to be more polyphagous and attack a much wider host range. *Macrolophus caliginosus* will live successfully on whitefly, leafhopper, leaf miner, spider mite, moth eggs and young caterpillar, and in the absence of suitable prey can survive on plant sap. Alone they can reduce a pest population to below economic damage levels or in some instances eliminate a pest completely. This particular predator can cause considerable yield losses on cherry tomato plants by feeding on pollen within the flowers after its prey has been consumed. It is then regarded as a major pest at certain times of the year.

INTEGRATED CROP AND PEST MANAGEMENT

However, in most situations more than one pest occurs at any one time and there are also plant diseases, weeds and nutritional disorders to contend with. Here IPM or ICM comes into action. IPM is the integration of biological control agents with selective pesticides and cultural control techniques (Sunderland *et al.*, 1992). ICM is as above but includes all aspects of crop production including selection of plants for pest or disease resistance, fertilizer use and environmental control where appropriate.

Cultural control includes polythene-covered floors to reflect light to the crop and also prevent weeds or volunteer plants which may require herbicide treatment, and sticky traps used to monitor and help control flying insects. These IPM techniques are available to amateur and professional growers alike and with skill work extremely well. The majority of cucumber, sweet pepper and tomato crop grown in protected environments in the UK are grown using full IPM programmes to control all the pests.

Most naturally occurring beneficial insects are only active during the summer months, they over-winter in a protected environment to reappear when temperatures and daylight hours increase. This usually corresponds to several weeks after the pest species have started their reproductive cycle and sufficient prey exists for their survival. Therefore, if biological control agents are to be used successfully they must be provided with the appropriate conditions: average temperature of 14°C (57°F) or above (lower temperatures will not kill but will slow their development), pest organisms in low numbers and usually sufficient hours of light to maintain activity. Most IPM programmes start in heated crops almost immediately the crop is planted, but in unheated crops the start may need to be delayed until early spring.

DEVELOPMENT OF GLASSHOUSE BIOLOGICAL CONTROL

Glasshouse biological control really started when the whitefly parasitoid *Encarsia formosa* was first used commercially in the late 1920s, following its discovery in a tomato crop and research into breeding methods in southern England. During the 1930s it was mass-produced and exported to several countries around the world. The spider mite predator *Phytoseiulus persimilis* entered the scene in 1960 when, in Germany, Dr. Dosse found it with spider mites on a consignment of orchids from Chile (Hussey, 1985).

Development of biological control all but ceased between the discovery of *Encarsia* and *Phytoseiulus* spp. This was due to the Second World War and subsequent widespread use of organochlorine pesticides such as dichlorodiphenyl-trichloroethane (DDT) and discovery of organophosphate insecticides. These were broad-spectrum, long-persistence products that initially controlled most pests for several weeks or months after a single application. Pest resistance and environmental concerns led to a resurgence of interest in

17 Sticky traps used to monitor the population of pests such as whitefly.

18 Ripening tomato fruit.

biological control methods. *Encarsia* and *Phytoseiulus* spp. were once again being used in research programmes and soon became available commercially to tomato and cucumber growers. The invention of synthetic pyrethroids in the early 1970s (Elliott *et al.*, 1973) and their widespread use by the end of that decade again slowed development of natural enemies. However, reports of whitefly becoming resistant to massive doses of pyrethroid insecticides soon brought biological control back in demand.

Minor pests, which had previously been easily controlled by pesticides, now became more of a problem. The lack of selective pesticides (those that kill a pest without undue harm to a beneficial) led to a wider range of natural enemies being used. The mass production of new beneficial insects required new techniques and methods to distribute them, as well as how best to integrate the biologicals together. Growing methods changed from soil to rockwool and hydroponics, which also led to a change in pest status for some insects. Cucumber was traditionally grown on wet straw bales, an environment generally too boggy for thrips to build up to seriously damaging levels, as they pupate on the ground. Change this to a clean, dry, polythene-covered floor and several diseases become more easily controlled but thrips become a major pest problem. The predatory mite *Amblyseius (Neoseiulus) cucumeris* was known about for many years and indeed frequently entered crops naturally, but there was a need to introduce many thousands at one time to achieve adequate pest control. Thus combined efforts by research teams and commercial producers developed the Controlled Release System (CRS) for use on cucumbers. Small sachets contain a breeding population of *A. cucumeris* and a source of food in the form of a bran mite and are placed one to a plant and release predators over a 6–8 week period. Subsequent research has shown that these sachets can be successfully used on a range of crops including ornamental plants, where their use on hanging baskets is extremely useful.

New control agents and methods to use them continue to be developed while new selective pesticides take much longer and cost considerably more. One of the latest developments is the use of insect parasitic nematodes which swim in the film of water that surrounds soil particles. Leaves freshly sprayed with water allow the nematodes to swim over that surface (Piggott *et al.*, 2000). In this way parasitic nematodes can be used as a living pesticide to control leaf miner larvae within the leaf and scale insects and thrips on the leaf.

19 A typical hanging card for distributing the whitefly parasitoid *Encarsia formosa*.

20 A mixed garden with vegetables, shrubs, trees, flowers and a glasshouse (photograph courtesy of Rosie Mayer/Holt Studios).

21 A well stocked garden glasshouse (photograph courtesy of Rosie Mayer/Holt Studios).

Practical Tips for Gardeners

In Section One of the book we have described three types of growing environment, representing three degrees of 'management' – arable crops, fruit growing and the protected or covered environment. Very often all three exist in the private garden. The notes below are intended to help the gardener create the right environment for biological control of pests and, incidentally, to make best use of the book.

SUITABLE HABITATS
Creating refuges or providing suitable habitats for biological controls is something the cottage gardener has been doing for generations. Here are some examples:

- A patch of yellow flowering Goldenrod (*Solidago*, family: Compositae) will encourage hoverflies to remain in the garden.
- The presence of early flowering, pollen producing plants will allow predatory mites and insects to establish themselves in high enough numbers to prevent major pest outbreaks. Plants from the Compositae or Asteraceae families seem to be most suitable for this purpose and include Coltsfoot (*Tussilago farfara*) and Michaelmas daisy (*Aster* spp.). Many of the Umbelliferae such as fennel (*Foeniculum vulgare*), angelica (*Angelica archangelica*), carrot (*Daucus corota*) and parsnip (*Pastinaca sativa*) are grown for medicinal and food uses, but all provide an excellent source of nutrition for beneficial insects (beware, some flowering Umbelliferae can be irritating to the skin).
- A small, contained area of wild plants such as nettles (*Urtica dioica*) is ideal for aphids that in turn provide food for ladybirds and parasitoids.
- Some dead wood, ideally with loose bark, will provide a suitable over-wintering site for adult ladybirds and other beetles. Loosely packed straw in a flowerpot or a small bundle of corrugated cardboard hung in a dry shed or garage will provide a similar over-wintering refuge for adult lacewings and ladybirds.
- Large colonies of aphids, as can appear during the spring months, produce sticky honeydew laden with kairomones that attract and feed many parasitoids and predators. Biological control organisms are therefore encouraged to locate the pest, feed and reproduce. Subsequent generations of beneficial organisms can then provide sustained pest control for the whole season.
- Allow nature to take its course and several different types of biological control organisms providing free pest management will (usually) reward you.

PARASITOIDS, PREDATORS AND PATHOGENS
The 3-Ps of pest control frequently pull together to reduce further pest attack. Here are two examples:

- Caterpillars. One or two will make a few small holes or stitch some leaves together, but a whole colony can devastate complete plants, rendering them inedible to humans. Several natural biological control organisms exist and, even after the severest pest attack from which many adults may have survived to fly away, there are likely to be some that have succumbed to nature. Moth eggs attacked by the minute *Trichogramma* spp. wasp change to a much darker colour; caterpillars may be attacked by numerous parasitoid wasps or eaten by predators.
- Viral or bacterial infection. Specific pathogens often provide the greatest degree of control by infecting whole populations and spreading as an epizootic infection. Once the biological control has been found and identified, better utilization and improved pest control can be established. All too frequently a broad-spectrum pesticide will be sprayed that should kill the pest, but will undoubtedly kill the natural enemies as well. This will reduce the number of natural enemies that can survive to help reduce further pest outbreaks.

PEST MONITORING
By monitoring pests visually on the plants, or by using coloured or pheromone-baited sticky traps, gardeners quickly discover when a particular flying pest is making a start on their plants. A hand lens or magnifying glass is one of the most important tools a gardener can have; 8–10× power is ideal. Close inspection of pest colonies can often reveal the eggs of a predator or the first signs of parasitoid activity. Further inspection over a period of days will show biological control in action.

We hope this book will go some way towards helping to identify what is present in nature, and aid the private gardener and commercial grower alike in their battle against pests. Using the book as a reference or as an educational tool, the good guys can be differentiated from the bad ones.

How many people recognize a ladybird larva as an aphid predator and not as a small alligator-shaped insect that should be squashed?

SECTION 2:
PEST PROFILES

- PEST IDENTIFICATION GUIDE
- COMMON PEST SPECIES

The pest profiles are a guide to the hosts that feed the biological control agents for which this book was written. In most instances any natural enemy would be closely associated with its host pest so this chapter should aid the identification of friend or foe. The organisms included here are representative of the major pest species found throughout the world that unwittingly fall victim to the beneficial organisms that feed in, or on them. It was felt essential to provide the family characteristics of the pests along with damage symptoms, life cycle and an indication of the beneficials that may be found attacking them. Our so called 'pest organisms' feed on plant or animal tissue and in most instances cause economic damage requiring some form of control. Some pests may be found in an alien environment such as on houseplants growing in offices or shopping malls; these tend to have pests appropriate to the environment that may not normally be present locally. In most natural environments there are natural enemies that use the pest species as part of their diet, and usually produce equilibrium to prevent excessive damage. It is now possible to initiate and even fully control many pests by introducing mass-produced biological control agents, often in place of, or integrated with, chemical pesticide sprays.

Pest Identification Guide

WITH SOME EXAMPLES OF BENEFICIAL SPECIES (SEE INDEX ON PAGE 27)

Plant damage symptoms	Pest	Pest characteristics
Round holes in leaves or notches around edge of leaf, whole plants destroyed in severe infestation. Weak growth, pot plants may appear over-watered, holes in tubers with grub inside.	**Beetles** (*grubs and adults*) 	Adults have hard outer skin, may fly when disturbed, all colours including metallic sheen. Larva usually creamy white and hidden in soil or within plant tissue, six small legs behind head.

Predators and pathogens

Predatory bug (*Podisus* spp.) Ground beetles (Carabidae) Fungal pathogens (various)

| Regular notches on edge of leaf, weak growth, wilting plants, grubs in compost. | **Vine weevil**  | Creamy white, 'C'-shaped grubs with shiny brown head, 1–10 mm in length. Adult is black with small light tan spots, hard body, 8 mm in length. |

Predators and pathogens

Ground beetles (Carabidae) Nematodes (*Steinernema* and *Heterorhabditis*)

Plant damage symptoms	Pest	Pest characteristics

Small 1 mm white spots on leaves, irregular lines/tunnels within leaf. Small puparium on leaf.

Leaf miner

Small, creamy white larvae 0.5–3 mm within leaf, grey/white blister-like pupa on underside of leaf or golden brown to black puparium on lower leaves and floor.

Parasitoids and predators

Parasitoid wasp (*Diglyphus* spp.)   Parasitoid wasp (*Dacnusa* spp.)   Predatory bug (*Macrolophus* spp.)

Weak plants, particularly during propagation, little or no root growth. Can spread root pathogens easily.

Sciarid (*fungus gnat fly/larvae*)

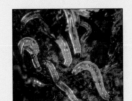

Small 2.5 mm flies black with transparent wings, frequently run over compost surface. Larvae in compost 0.5–2.5 mm, transparent with shiny black head.

Predators and pathogens

 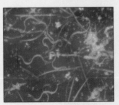  

Predatory mite (*Hypoaspis miles*)   Nematode (*Steinernema* spp.)   Fungal pathogens (various)   Predatory rove beetle (*Atheta coriaria*)

Yellowing of leaves, sticky deposit on lower leaves, giving rise to sooty-mould. Small, white bodied flies and scales (larvae) on underside of leaves.

Whitefly

Adults 1.5–2 mm white to grey. Usually at top of plant. Larvae are small 0.2–1.5 mm 'scales', white to creamy yellow on underside of leaves.

Parasitoids, predators and pathogens

 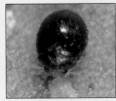   

Predatory bug (*Macrolophus* spp.)   Ladybird (*Delphastus* spp.)   Parasitoid wasp (*Encarsia formosa*)   Parasitoid wasp (*Eretmocerus* spp.)   Fungal pathogens (various)

Plant damage symptoms	Pest	Pest characteristics
Yellow patches on leaves, distorted growth, rolled leaves, sticky residue with white skins, sooty-mould.	**Aphids and Psyllids** (*greenfly, blackfly and plant suckers*) 	Variable colour, light to dark green, brown to black, 1–3 mm, some adults may be winged. Found on stem, shoots and underside of leaves.

Parasitoids, predators and pathogens

Ground beetles (Carabidae)	Ladybirds (Coccinellidae)	Rove beetles (*Tachyporus* spp.)	Empid flies (Empididae)	Predatory midges (*Aphidoletes* spp.)

  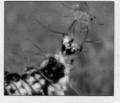  

Hoverflies (Syrphidae)	Predatory bugs (Anthocoridae)	Lacewings (Chrysopidae)	Parasitoid wasps (various)	Fungal pathogens (various)

Irregular white patches on leaves 1–5 mm diameter joining together to form chains of bleached white damage.	**Leafhoppers** 	Very mobile grey/white to green nymphs 0.5–3 mm long. Winged adults 3.5–5 mm, fly and jump when disturbed.

Parasitoids and predators

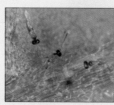 

Parasitoid wasp (*Anagrus* spp.)	Predatory bug (*Macrolophus* spp.)

Plant damage symptoms	Pest	Pest characteristics
Yellow leaves and stems, white cottony deposit, sticky residue, sooty-mould.	**Mealybugs** 	Pink to white waxy bodies, segmented 1–4 mm long, some have pairs of waxy tails.

Parasitoids and predators

Australian ladybird (*Cryptolaemus* spp.)	Parasitoid wasp (*Leptomastix* spp.)	Lacewings (Chrysopidae)

| Yellow patches/spots on leaves, sticky residue/sooty-mould on upper surface of lower leaves. | **Scale insects**  | Light green to black, flat bodies, scales or domed hard bodied or white oyster-like layers 'concertinered' on top of each other up to 15 mm long. |

Parasitoids and predators

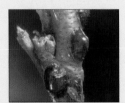 

Ladybird (*Chilocorus* spp.)	Parasitoid wasp (*Metaphycus* spp.)

| Irregular holes/'windows' in leaves, fruit damaged, leaves and shoots folded together. | **Caterpillars** (*moth or butterfly larvae*) 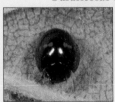 | Narrow insects 1–50 mm long. Variable in colour and markings, three pairs of legs in front half of body, additional two to five pairs of thicker walking legs at rear. |

Parasitoids, predators and pathogens

Predatory bug (*Podisus* spp.)	Parasitoid wasp (*Cotesia* spp.)	Parasitoid wasp (*Trichogramma* spp.)	Entomopathogen (*Bacillus thuringiensis*)	Entomopathogen (Baculoviruses)

Plant damage symptoms	Pest	Pest characteristics

Silvery speckling on leaves or flowers, streaks of lost colour in flowers, distorted growth, senescence, virus transmission.

Thrips (*thunder bugs*)

Small, narrow bodies 0.5–2.5 mm long, creamy yellow to golden brown or black, winged adults.

Predators

Predatory mite (*Amblyseius* [*Iphiseius*] *degenerans*) | Predatory mite (*Amblyseius* [*Neoseiulus*] *cucumeris*) | Predatory mite (*Amblyseius* [*Typhlodromips*] *montdorensis*) | Predatory bugs (*Orius* spp.) | Lacewings (Chrysopidae)

Tiny yellow spots that converge to form large yellow patches, can lead to death of leaf, loss of yield and death of plant.

Spider mites
(*red- or 2-spotted spider mites*)

Adults 1 mm, light to dark green to orange to carmine red. Eggs 0.2 mm diameter, nymphs mobile but have two resting stages.

Predators

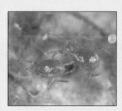
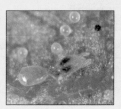

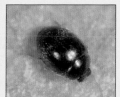

Predatory mite (*Phytoseiulus* spp.) | Predatory mite (*Amblyseius* spp.) | Predatory mite (*Typhlodromus* spp.) | Predatory midge (*Feltiella* spp.) | Minute black ladybird (*Stethorus* spp.)

Rough edged holes in flat leaves, rolled leaves can open with line of small holes made when pest eats through whole leaf. Fruit can be eaten, decaying vegetation often eaten. Shiny slime trail left on plants, paths and other hard surfaces.

Slugs and snails (*molluscs*)

Unsegmented body, four tentacles on the head, snails have shell in which the body can retract, slugs have no shell. Slimy feel to body. Often found in damp areas.

Predators and pathogens

Ground beetles (Carabidae) | Centipedes (Chilopoda) | Parasitic nematode (*Phasmarhabditis* spp.)

Plant damage symptoms	Pest	Pest characteristics
Irregular holes in leaves, usually lower leaves touching the ground are more severely damaged. Feeding can resemble slug damage but without the slime trail.	**Woodlice** (*sow or pill bugs*) 	Usually grey, 2.5–18 mm in length, several segments to the body with 14 legs. Pill bugs roll into a characteristic ball when disturbed, hide in damp places.

Predators

Ground beetles   Centipedes   Spiders
(Carabidae)   (Chilopoda)   (Arachnidae)

Common Pest Species

BEETLES
ORDER: COLEOPTERA (22–26)

This is the largest order of insects with over a million known species being found throughout the world, some able to survive in extreme environments. Predatory beetles are described in more detail through the pages of this book, this section will deal briefly with some of the plant damaging species. Vine weevil, as one of the more common and serious pest insects is profiled separately on the next pages. All beetles have biting mouth-parts capable of chewing into hard surfaces, such as seed grains, most leaves, insect bodies, roots, stems and live or dead wood. In most species, it is the larva that is most damaging; they too have biting jaws and usually feed on similar food to the adult.

Some of the more common pest species living in soil and feeding on plant roots are from the Scarabaeidae which include chafer grubs and chafer beetles. These have a life cycle spanning 1–3 or more years, adults are usually found from late spring to early summer and once mated the females burrow into friable, free draining soil to lay eggs. These hatch soon after to larva that feed mainly on grass roots but will equally feed on, and damage, roots of lettuce, strawberry and several ornamental shrubs. Larvae feed to a depth of 5–15 cm until late autumn when they burrow deeper and produce an earthen cell in which they over-winter. Pupation occurs within the cell during spring to produce fresh adults the following season. Predatory ground beetles provide reasonable control but in areas where natural enemies have been depleted such as golf courses, heavy pesticide use has been necessary. Recent trials with insect parasitoid nematodes as used for vine weevil control have been successful and are more environmentally friendly.

Beetles from the family Elateridae are known as click beetles or skip-jacks after their ability to flick themselves in the air with an audible click when they fall on their backs. The larvae are known as wireworms and can cause considerable damage to many plant roots in the garden, on grasses or, more rarely, in agricultural crops. Permanent grasslands contain the greatest populations of click beetles and most damage is done when these areas are used for arable crops. The larvae possess six almost invisible legs and have a firm, cylindrical body covered with a tough skin, and a dark brown head with powerful biting mouth-parts to eat into many host plant roots and stems. They may spend 4–5 years as larvae before developing to a pupa and then adult the following spring. The principal beneficial organisms that attack wireworms include birds, several predatory beetle larvae and insect pathogenic fungi.

The family of beetles known as the Chrysomelidae are mostly leaf feeders and include the tiny flea beetle that bores small holes in leaves. Most flea beetles are very host plant specific and when a particularly favoured plant is grown on any form of commercial scale severe economic losses can occur. Due to their voracious appetite and potential narrow host range flea beetles are now successfully used for the biological control of several weed species in Canada and the USA.

Colorado potato beetle is one of the most infamous Chrysomelidae that may be found across Canada and the USA and several areas of Europe. Its principal food plant is potato but severe damage can be done to aubergine, pepper and tomato. Both larva and adults feed on leaves of Solanaceae and can lead to plant death. Colorado potato beetle is notorious due to its ability to gain resistance rapidly to pesticides applied for its control. **Predatory shield bugs of *Podisus* spp. are now being used in several countries with good success. Similarly, other biological controls such as *Bacillus thuringiensis* are becoming more widely used against this pest.**

22 *Melolontha melolontha* (Linnaeus) (cockchafer) larva.

23 *Agriotes* sp. (wireworm or click beetle larva) and damage to a potato tuber.

24 Larva of *Leptinotarsa decemlineata* (Say) (Colorado beetle) on a potato crop, Prince Edwards Island, Canada.

25 An adult *L. decemlineata*.

26 *Phyllotretes nemorum* (Linnaeus) (turnip flea beetle) adult.

WEEVILS
ORDER: COLEOPTERA; FAMILY CURCULIONIDAE (27, 28)

This is the main family of weevils and deserves special mention due to the widespread nature of damage done to many household, nursery and soft fruit plants. Many species are native to Europe and are an introduced pest to North America where damage ranging from 'troublesome' to severe economic, is recorded on several crops. *Otiorhynchus sulcatus* is commonly known as the black vine weevil, cyclamen borer or strawberry root weevil and is found on many horticultural crops throughout the temperate regions of the world. Other species such as *O. singularis* (Linnaeus) and *O. rugosostriatus* (Goez) (clay coloured and lesser strawberry weevil, respectively) have similar life cycles but are smaller at all stages than *O. sulcatus*. Economic damage can be produced by a single weevil larva feeding on a cyclamen corm to several larvae that may kill or weaken quite mature plants. Adults are nocturnal feeders of leaves and produce a characteristic edge notching which in itself may cause economic damage to ornamental plants. In outdoor or unheated crops there is usually only one generation each year but in heated conservatories, botanic gardens and interior atriums there may be overlapping generations. All recorded adult vine weevils have been female; males are thought to have died out during the last Ice Age, so reproduction is entirely parthenogenetic.

Adults are wingless and 7–10 mm in length; migration is limited when compared to many other insects although plant movement by man accounts for most of its rapid colonization. Eggs are laid on the compost surface, initially soft white and glistening they melanize to become rigid and reddish-brown in colour. The newly hatched or neonate larva is white and legless with a brown head; older larva normally have a 'C' shape and may acquire some colour from their host plant. Mature larvae may begin to burrow into corms and fleshy stems of several plant species where they are well protected from most forms of control, including pesticides. Larvae overwinter in cells produced in the compost and remain dormant until warmer conditions return and feeding activity resumes. After the final larval instar is reached a pupal cell is formed and the weevil pupates, emerging some weeks later as an adult.

Natural enemies of vine weevil include insectivorous mammals (hedgehogs and moles), several birds, frogs, toads, lizards and predatory insects such as carabid beetles. Entomopathogenic fungi such as *Beauveria bassiana* and *Metarhizium anisopliae* and entomopathogenic nematodes such as *Heterorhabditis megidis*, *Steinernema carpocapsae* and *S. kraussei* are commercially available.

27 *Otiorhychus sulcatus* (Fabricius) (vine weevil) larvae.

28 *O. sulcatus* adult.

LEAF MINERS
ORDER: DIPTERA; FAMILY: AGROMYZIDAE (29–32)

Larvae mine between the laminar of leaves and, in severe infestations, they can tunnel in flowers and plant stems, killing developing growth. Apart from disfiguring ornamental plants, high numbers of mines can lead to economic loss of vegetable and salad crops. Adult females (2.5–3 mm long) wound leaves with their ovipositor leaving open pits from which both sexes feed on plant juices; in some pits an egg is deposited. This hatches to a minute larva, which begins tunnelling in the leaf forming a characteristic mine. In some species the mine is spiral or serpentine while others produce mines which follow the leaf veins. The mine shape and frass trail within can help differentiate species of leaf miner.

Mature larva (3–3.5 mm long) can either pupate in the leaf as a small blister, usually on the underside of mined leaves, or drop out of the leaf to produce a puparium, depending on species. Those that pupate externally may land on the upper surface of lower leaves or drop through to the soil where they may remain for several months while they over-winter. **Leaf miner larvae may be parasitized by specialized wasps, predated on by heteropteran bugs or eaten as pupae by ground beetles. Adult leaf miner flies can be caught on yellow sticky traps, with horizontal traps catching considerably more than vertically hung ones.**

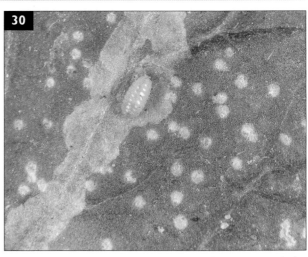

30 *L. huidobrensis* pupa and adult puncture holes in a tomato leaf.

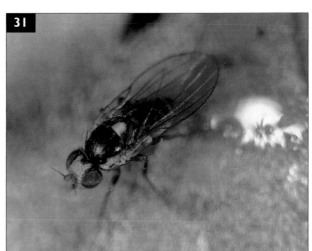

31 *L. huidobrensis* adult fly.

29 *Liriomyza huidobrensis* (Blanchard) (South American leaf miner) damage to a tomato crop.

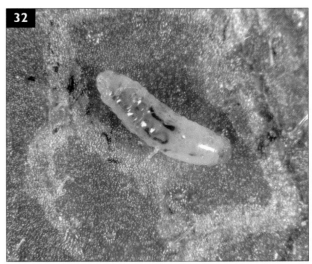

32 *Liriomyza trifolii* (Burgess) (serpentine leaf miner) larva.

SCIARIDS
ORDER: DIPTERA; FAMILY: SCIARIDAE (**33–35**)

Commonly known as fungus gnats, the narrow black fly (2.5 mm long) runs over the surface of compost and deposits eggs just below the surface. The larvae are almost transparent with a shiny black head and can reach up to 6 mm in length before pupating close to the compost surface. Black and white threads inside the larva are the gut and fat deposits. Larvae feed on young root tissue, stunting the plant growth; cuttings can be tunnelled like a drinking straw often leading to its death. Both adults and larvae can exacerbate root pathogens such as *Pythium* and *Thieliviopsis* spp. which cause seedlings to 'damp off'; adults by direct carrying and larvae by creating an entry point for the disease. Moist composts with a high organic matter content are most favoured although it is not uncommon to find them in rockwool or even hydroponic growing systems.

Control of sciarid larvae can be achieved by predatory mites (*Hypoaspis* spp.), parasitoid nematodes, parasitoid wasps, pathogenic bacteria (specific strains of *Bacillus thuringiensis*) or entomopathogenic fungi (*Conidiobolus* spp.). The latter are naturally occurring and leave the dead larva resembling a thread of cotton on the compost surface.

Many growers mistake fungus gnats for shore flies (*Scatella stagnalis*), family: Ephydridae, which are slightly longer (3 mm long) and broader (1.25 mm wide) as adult flies. When at rest either on a plant, compost or other flat surface their folded wings appear to have three white spots across them. *Scatella* spp. feed mainly on algae but the larvae may cause slight damage to roots. Adults sitting on leaves may leave black faecal spots that on edible crops such as herbs cause cosmetic and health concerns. The larvae are white and segmented with a small black head; they feed in and on algae that may be growing on almost any surface including compost, benches, paths and floors where conditions allow algae to establish. A hard skinned puparium develops in the algae and depending on temperatures the adult may emerge after only 3–4 days, giving rise to rapidly increasing populations. **Control is best achieved by eliminating their algae food source with proprietary algaecides. Biological controls as above for sciarids may have a limited effect on *Scatella* spp. control.**

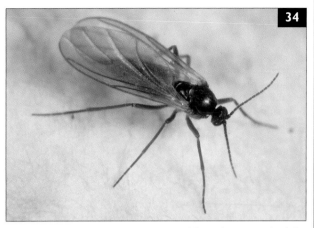

34 *Lycoriella auripila* (Winnertz) (sciarid fly or fungus gnat) adult.

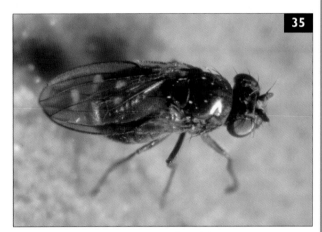

35 *Scatella stagnalis* (Fallén) (shore fly) adult.

33 *Lycoriella* sp. (sciarid fly or fungus gnat) larvae.

ORDER HEMIPTERA

All Hemiptera possess piercing mouth-parts made up of needle-like mandibles that penetrate the outer layer of cells. In plant feeding species, the mandibles probe deep into the tissues to feed on sap. In doing so, they transfer some of their saliva that begins the digestion process; the saliva may carry plant viruses that enter as the pest feeds. Plant sap is relatively poor in the amino acids that are needed by the insect to develop, but they are rich in sugars. This accounts for large quantities of a sugary waste product, called honeydew, being deposited over the leaves of some plants. A *Cladosporium* fungus can grow on the honeydew resulting in a black sooty-mould that excludes light from reaching the leaves and severely interrupts photosynthesis. In this way, plant damage can manifest itself in several forms, often producing serious economic losses. **However, as this order has so many pest species that are commonly found throughout the world they frequently form the diet of many parasitoid and predatory insects. Several entomopathogenic fungi and some mites also kill these insects. Some of the parasitoids are exclusive to just a few species while, in general, predators will feed on many species and even other insects.**

WHITEFLY
ORDER: HEMIPTERA; FAMILY: ALEYRODIDAE
(36–40)

The presence of whitefly detracts from the plant value; they can transmit several plant viruses and in high numbers can produce copious quantities of honeydew to leaves and fruit on which a sooty-mould fungus can grow. They are common on a range of protected and field vegetable crops throughout the world. In cotton and field grown tomato crops whole clouds of adult whitefly, usually a *Bemisia* strain, may be disturbed and found on the wing at one time. The *Bemisia* genus is probably the most economically damaging of the whiteflies and is now divided into various strains (A, B and so on) and even new species that reflect the nature of the crop damage inflicted on plants (*Bemisia argentifolii* [Bellows and Perring] = silver leaf whitefly). Pesticide resistance is frequent in many populations; however, some of the new, specific insecticides offer better control and with current resistance strategies in practice should remain active for several years.

Adults are small (1.25–2 mm), grey to white winged flies. Some species have bands or spots on their wings, and they are usually found at rest on the underside of leaves. Eggs are initially white and laid in semi-circles; after a few days they melanize to an almost black colour before hatching to a six-legged nymph. This 'crawler' stage moves a short distance to locate a suitable site for larval development. The four larval instars are commonly known as whitefly scales and may take between 7 and 20 days to develop. The last part of the fourth instar in referred to as a pupal stage, although as no molt occurs it is a false pupal stage. In some species the 'pupa' may be covered in a waxy secretion making it difficult to see clearly. Adults emerge some ten days later and start to feed almost immediately and oviposition usually begins 1–2 days later. Adult whitefly may live for several weeks.

Whitefly may be parasitized by specialized wasps, predated on by heteropteran bugs and cocinellids or infected by several entomopathogenic fungi. Yellow traps are also useful in reducing high numbers of adult whiteflies, but may also catch natural enemies.

37 *Bemisia tabaci* (Gennadius) (cotton whitefly) severe infestation of scales and pupae on a phaseolus bean leaf.

38 *B. tabaci* courting pair.

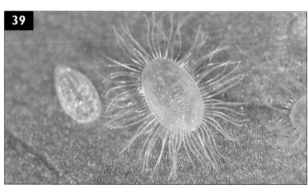

39 *Trialeurodes ricini* (Misra) (castor whitefly) scale and pupa.

36 *Trialeurodes vaporariorum* (Westwood) (glasshouse whitefly) adults on tomato leaves.

40 *Aleyrodes proletella* (Linnaeus) (cabbage whitefly) female with her eggs.

APHIDS
ORDER: HEMIPTERA; FAMILY: APHIDIDAE (41–44)
Commonly known as blackfly, greenfly, greenbug and plant lice, aphids are small soft-bodied insects ranging in size from 0.5 mm to about 6.5 mm in length. Colours can vary between different species and even between strains of the same species, ranging from shades of green through to black, yellow, chestnut brown, pink, grey and waxy white. Several species have darker markings on a lighter toned body, camouflaging them against their plant background but aiding identification for us. Aphids may be differentiated from other Hemiptera by the ability to produce active young (viviparous birth) from unimpregnated females (parthenogenesis); the same species may be present as alate (winged) and apterae (wingless) simultaneously on the same leaf. Alate aphids are frequently produced in response to adverse conditions such as overcrowding, poor plant condition, the onset of winter conditions or for migratory purposes

The biological life cycle of aphids can be one of three types: 1. *Monoecious holocycle*, which is the simplest and most common on outdoor crops, where all the generations develop on the same host plant species. Over-wintered eggs hatch to parthenogenetic females in the spring. These produce both alate and apterous aphids through the summer months and a sexual generation in the autumn that after mating lay eggs to survive the winter. 2. *Dioecious holocycle* where the aphid has two different host plants, a woody winter host in which eggs are laid to over-winter and a vegetative summer host that supports the bulk of generations. Usually two generations occur after the eggs hatch in the spring followed by a migration to the main summer host plant on which multiple generations (both winged and wingless) are produced. As above, a sexual generation develops in the autumn that migrates back to the winter plant for egg production. 3. *Anholocyclic* in which no sexuals are produced and so no eggs laid, all the aphids being parthenogenetic females as alate or apterae depending on plant condition and colony density. This type is common in the Mediterranean, sub-tropical and tropical regions where winter conditions are very mild to non-existent; they also occur on many protected crops.

Aphids feed by penetrating the plant tissue with four ultra thin stylets that are held within a protective rostrum, which at rest is folded against the underside of the insect. Only the stylets enter the plant as the insect feeds, injecting saliva by way of a small canal formed between the hypodermic-like stylets and sucking up the partially digested sap. During feeding aphids (and many other sap feeding insects) can transmit numerous plant viruses, cause galls to form or leaves to roll around the pest colony. Large volumes of sap are taken in during feeding and almost equal amounts of sugary water excreted as honeydew. This is flicked away from the aphid to fall on the upper surface of leaves and stems. High numbers of aphids can give rise to copious quantities of sticky honeydew, which in turn can become infected with a fungus turning the whole area black with sooty-mould. Ants are frequently associated with aphids and may assumed to be feeding on the insect when they are in fact feeding on the sugary honeydew.

Aphids are very common and numerous, and are a major source of biological control nutrition. They are parasitized by several hymenoptera wasps, predated on by almost every group of insect and mite predator, and are attacked by several fungal pathogens.

41 *Aphis fabae* (Scopdi) (black bean aphid) colony.

43 *Rhopalosiphum padi* (Linnaeus) (bird-cherry aphid), a vector for barley yellow dwarf virus shown on the wheat leaf here.

42 *Metapolophium dirhodum* (Walker) (rose–grain aphid) female with offspring.

44 *Aulacorthum circumflexum* (Buckton) (mottled arum aphid) clearly showing the stylet used to penetrate the plant tissue.

LEAFHOPPERS
ORDER: HEMIPTERA; FAMILY:CICADELLIDAE (45–47)

Adults and nymphs resemble elongated aphids but can be much more mobile, particularly in the older life stages; adults are easily disturbed and with a short flight jump between leaves and plants. Adult size varies from 2.5 mm to 10 mm depending on species. They can also be very colourful with spots, stripes and dapples aiding their camouflage amongst leaves. Feeding is by the insertion of a proboscis that sucks sap; air enters the empty plant cells and gives rise to the visible symptoms. Plant damage varies between leaf type, soft leaves showing the most serious in the form of short yellow/white chains leading to almost completely bleached leaves, as can occur on chrysanthemum, salvia and tomato. Harder leaves such as rhododendron and fruit trees tend to show less visible damage except where very high numbers occur. Females lay up to 50 eggs singly into veins on the underside of leaves that hatch after 5–10 days to minute wingless nymphs, which can take up to two months to reach adulthood. The common name 'ghost fly' has been given to leafhopper due to the rapid appearance of damage and only a transparent skin left on the leaf, this being the cast skins of nymphs that are attached to the leaf by the insect's proboscis. Feeding on young seedlings can lead to plant death while damage to older plants is mainly cosmetic. Several species are responsible for virus transmission.

The egg parasitoids *Anagrus* spp. are commercially available in some countries but most control of leafhopper is by predators such as lacewings (*Chrysoperla* spp.), ladybirds (*Coccinella* spp.) and anthocorid bugs.

47 *Graphocephala fennahi* (Young) (rhododendron leafhopper) adult.

PSYLLIDS
ORDER: HEMIPTERA; FAMILY: PSYLLIDAE (48, 49)

Psyllids or suckers are small aphid-like insects. The adults have large membranous wings but they tend to jump rather than fly; most species are free living although some form galls in which eggs are laid. Trees such as alder, apple, ash, birch, box, eucalyptus, hawthorn and pear form the main host plant range. Psyllids tend to be host specific pests capable of causing considerable damage when they attack growing points and flowers. Nymphs are flattened and, in some species, with their slow movement resemble scale insects. They produce a white waxy secretion that covers and protects the nymphs; copious honeydew is also produced most of which remains in wax-covered droplets that prevent the insects becoming sticky. **Psyllids are better protected than aphids, but are attacked by lacewings, ladybirds and other generalist predators.**

45 *Hauptidia maroccana* (Melichar) (glasshouse leafhopper) nymphs.

46 *H. maroccana* adult.

48 *Psylla mali* (Schmidberger) (apple sucker) nymph.

49 *Psylla mali* (apple sucker) adult.

50 *Pseudococcus longispinus* (Targioni-Tazzetti) (long-tailed mealybug) infestation on a glasshouse palm.

MEALYBUGS
ORDER: HEMIPTERA; FAMILY: PSEUDOCOCCIDAE (50, 51)

Of tropical and sub-tropical origin these sap-sucking insects are now found on protected plants throughout the world, particularly on slow growing and permanently sited plants such as interior atriums. They are becoming a major pest on commercial tomato crops due to the length of the cropping cycle; frequently 48–50 weeks with a 2–4 week turn around before the next crop is introduced. In warmer regions mealybug can be found on several outdoor plants such as citrus and other orchard crops where severe economic damage may be caused. Their bodies are covered with dusty white wax filaments, some of which form a fringe around the insect. They are sap feeders and several species produce copious quantities of honeydew that encourages black sooty-mould. In high numbers stem girdling can kill branches or even whole plants. Toxins can be injected as mealybugs feed causing distortion and yellowing of foliage in some plants. Although mobile they tend to remain localized, frequently moving slowly along stems as the plant grows. Clumps of mealybug can become too heavy to support and fall to lower leaves or the ground where they disperse to start new colonies. Male mealybugs are delicate winged flies and are extremely rare; after repeatedly mating they die within 48 hours. Most reproduction is parthenogenetic with females of some species giving birth to live young while others produce masses of eggs covered in a protective white woolly wax.

The Australian ladybird *Cryptolaemus montrouzieri* is commercially used throughout most of the world and provides adequate control of several species. Specific parasitoids are becoming more widely available and can be used in association with predators. Other generalist predators such as lacewings are also found feeding on young nymphs; similarly predatory mites (*Hypoaspis* spp.) feed on root mealybug in compost and foliage species when close to the ground. Entomopathogenic fungi provide good control providing high enough humidities can be maintained to support the fungal infection.

51 *Planococcus citri* (Risso) (citrus mealybug) on an Easter cactus peduncle.

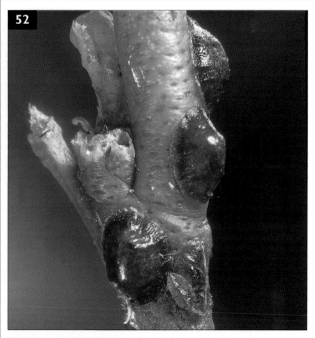

52 *Saisettia coffeae* (Walker) (hemispherical scale insect).

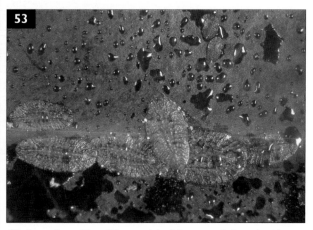

53 *Coccus hesperidum* (Linnaeus) (soft brown scale insect) with honeydew secretion on a houseplant leaf.

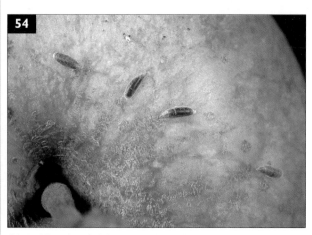

54 *Lepidosaphes ulmi* (Linnaeus) (mussel scale) on an apple fruit.

SCALE INSECTS
ORDER: HEMIPTERA; FAMILY: COCCIDAE AND DIASPIDIDAE (52–54)

Adults range in size from 3–7 mm and can be circular or elongated, all have a waxy skin that protects the body. Soft scale insects (Coccidae) produce honeydew, often in large quantities giving rise to sooty-mould, whereas armoured or hard scale insects (Diaspididae) do not. Scale insects are hardier than mealybugs and have a larger geographical range, being found on several outdoor plants throughout Europe and North America. They are most frequently associated with conservatory plants and in field situations on citrus. As with mealybugs, males are scarce so most reproduction is parthenogenetic; some species produce several hundred eggs while others are viviparous. Young nymphs are known as crawlers and can move several centimetres from their place of birth before settling to complete their development. Eggs and nymphs can also be transported on wind currents, in water droplets, by insects, birds and frequently by man. Plant damage can be seen as yellowing foliage, weakened or stunted growth, sunken spots that correspond to a mature scale insect on the underside of leaves (as can be found on banana) and the growth of sooty-mould from honeydew residues.

Several host specific parasitoids are associated with scale insects; the mealybug destroyer *Cryptolaemus* spp. will also feed on these pests as will lacewing larva and other generalist predators. Parasitoid nematodes used against vine weevil larvae have given excellent control when sprayed onto leaves (the leaf surface must remain wet for several hours after application for best results).

CATERPILLARS (MOTHS AND BUTTERFLIES)
ORDER: LEPIDOPTERA (55–59)

Caterpillars are the larval stages of moths and butterflies. In almost all species they are plant feeders, being equipped with powerful jaws capable of eating through most plant tissue, including roots, young stems, leaves, flowers and fruit. Damage may be seen as complete defoliation of a particularly favoured host plant or, more subtly, as a weakening of plants by root feeders and stem borers. Tortricid caterpillars protect themselves by feeding within rolled leaves or growing tips that are stitched together with a silken thread, while others from this family feed inside fruit such as the codling moth (*Cydia pomonella*) which is found in apples. Many Lepidoptera feed inside leaves and may be mistaken for leaf miners but they can easily be identified by their capability of producing silk from spinnerets found behind the head, used to escape attack by parasitoids or predators. The generally undifferentiated thorax (segments immediately behind the head) may bear a hard protective plate but always has three pairs of true legs (except in some of the leaf mining caterpillars where the first instar is often legless). The abdomen has 2–5 pairs of fleshy prolegs, used for walking as well as clinging onto surfaces, and the rear of the larva has an anal plate and an anal clasper. Caterpillar skin can be smooth, bristly or very hairy; the hairs are, in some species, irritating and act as a defence mechanism when the insect is attacked. Colour and body form can vary dramatically making both caterpillar and adult moth or butterfly extremely varied. Developing larvae must periodically shed their skins as they grow and once fully developed form a pupa. This is usually the over-wintering stage and the pupa may remain hidden for several months before the adult moth or butterfly emerges.

Many predators and parasitoids attack and kill caterpillars including parasitoid wasps (Hymenoptera) and parasitoid flies (Diptera) which lay their eggs inside young larvae; the minute *Trichogramma* spp. lay their eggs into the moth eggs. Predators include bugs (Hemiptera) such as Anthocoridae and lacewing larvae (Neuroptera). Birds and beetles will also devour caterpillars and pupae. Several pathogens attack Lepidoptera, these include bacteria of which *Bacillus thuringiensis* is the most widely found and commercially used form of biological control. Fungi and viruses are also common in some areas and are beginning to be used commercially due to their host insect specificity; usually it is the larval stage that is killed.

57 *Agrotis segetum* (Denis and Schiffermüller) (turnip cutworm) inside a damaged potato tuber.

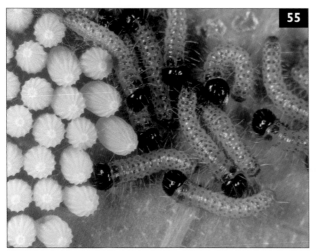

55 *Pieris brassicae* (Linnaeus) (large white butterfly) eggs and young caterpillars.

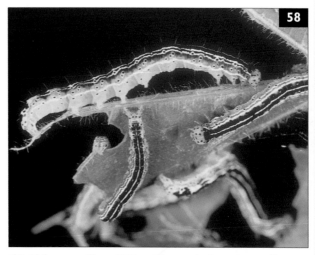

58 *Alabama argillacea* (Hübner) (cotton leafworm) caterpillars.

56 A savoy cabbage plant stripped by *P. brassicae* caterpillars.

59 *Helicoverpa armigera* (Hübner) (cotton bollworm) moth.

THRIPS
ORDER: THYSANOPTERA; FAMILY: THRIPIDAE (60–62)

Adults are tiny, winged insects ranging in colour from light golden yellow, brown (with and without stripes) to black with and without stripes. They have several common names including thunder bugs and thrips named for the plant or geographical region from which they originated. For instance, gladiolus thrips (*Thrips simplex*) a pest of gladioli flowers and western flower thrips (*Frankliniella occidentalis*), a pest which originated on the west coast of North America but is now found on many plants throughout the world. Thrips damage leaves, fruit and flowers by piercing and sucking out the cells of the surface membranes, leaving silvery/grey patches littered with small black fecal pellets. Leaf and fruit distortion can occur when thrips feed on very young, developing parts of the plant leading to severe economic losses. Several thrips species are also responsible for transmission of plant viruses, which can also lead to economic losses. In some countries and states certain species of thrips are notifiable; quarantine pests and their presence may to lead to crop destruction or more usually a chemical spray programme.

Adult females oviposit into plant tissue and may leave a small raised blister where the egg was laid. Eggs hatch after 2–12 days to minute first instar larva which last only a few days before moulting to second instar larva (4–10 days), these develop to prepupa and pupa. Pupal stages of thrips may occur on the plant or in the growing media below and can last for a few days to several months depending on temperatures. Adults have a pre-oviposition period of 2–10 days before they commence their next generation.

Predatory mites (*Hypoaspis* spp.) can kill thrip pupae if they pupate on the ground. Parasitoid nematodes, parasitoid wasps, predatory Hymenoptera and entomopathogenic fungi are commercially used to control larvae and adults. The most widely used control agents are *Amblyseius* species of mites that attack mainly the first instar larva and are routinely used as a preventive measure against thrip establishment.

61 *Thrips simplex* (Morison) (gladiolus thrips) nymphs.

62 *Frankliniella occidentalis* (Pergande) (western flower thrips) adult.

SPIDER MITES
ORDER: ARACHNIDA; FAMILY: TETRANYCHIDAE AND TARSONEMIDAE (63–68)

This order of organisms includes spiders, scorpions and ticks as well as the minute plant damaging mites commonly found speckling leaves on many crops throughout the world. High numbers of spider mites can distort young plants or completely desiccate leaves and flowers, by which time webbing can form on the apical growing points of plants and canes. The webbing is a mass of fine silken threads that starts to rain down with droplets of pure spider mites; these can be caught in air currents or transported mechanically (including by humans) to other plants.

The Tetranychidae are the larger mites up to 0.75 mm in length, usually yellow-green to dark red in colour. However, when conditions are unfavourable some species turn a bright orange-red and enter a diapause state, when feeding and egg production cease until more suitable conditions return. Under glasshouse conditions where good plant growth and reasonable temperatures (above 16°C [61°F]) can be maintained the mites are active through the year, although their life cycle is considerably slower at lower temperatures. Females produce up to 100 spherical eggs 0.14 mm in diameter, that are initially transparent but turn white to light yellow just prior to egg hatch. A six-legged larva emerges and feeds for a short while before settling on the leaf to form a protonymph; this may last a few days depending on temperature before developing into a deutonymph. At this

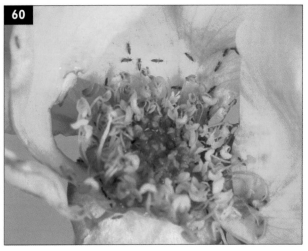

60 *Thrips fuscipennis* (Haliday) (rose thrips) in a rose flower.

stage females are distinguishable from males by their larger size and rounded shape, while males have a pointed rear and are much more active. Control may be species dependant with predatory mites such as *Phytoseiulus persimilis* providing good control of glasshouse spider mite (*Tetranychus urticae*) but limited control of fruit tree spider mite (*Panonychus ulmi*) which is controlled by *Typhlodromus pyri*. The midge predator *Feltiella acarisuga* is more polyphagous and will attack most spider mites; other predators include lacewings, mirids (*Macrolophus* spp.), anthocorids and entomopathogenic fungi.

Tarsonemid mites are much smaller and, at about 0.25 mm in length, are easily overlooked. The more commonly found species include bulb scale mites, cyclamen/strawberry mites and broad mites. Damage usually occurs on young growth in the form of distorted leaves, frequently discoloured with a shiny appearance. The mites are slow moving and creamy light brown in colour. Eggs are laid on the leaf or flower surface and hatch to a six-legged larva which, after feeding for a few days, enters a resting stage. Male broad mites (and some other species) may be seen carrying a resting stage female nymph on their backs using a pair of anal claspers that release the female when she matures and they mate. **The predatory mite *Hypoaspis* spp. is used for bulb scale mite control and *Amblyseius cucumeris* for leaf or flower feeding tarsonemid mites; other predatory mites are likely to feed on these pest mites but their efficacy has not been determined.**

65 *T. urticae* adults on webbing.

66 *Panonychus ulmi* (Koch) (fruit tree red spider mite) eggs overwintering on apple wood.

63 *Tetranychus urticae* (Koch) (2-spotted spider mite) damage and webbing on a french bean.

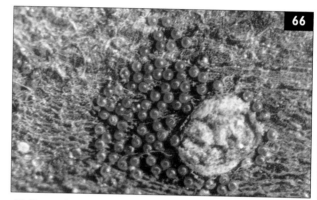

67 *P. ulmi* adult female.

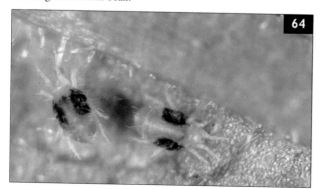

64 *T. urticae* adult females.

68 *Phytonemus pallidus* (Banks) (strawberry tarsonemid mites).

SLUGS AND SNAILS
PHYLUM: MOLLUSCA; CLASS GASTROPODA (69–71)

Land molluscs are traditionally divided into two categories, slugs and snails; those without an external shell or having one which is very small in relation to the body are slugs and those which can retreat into a protective shell being snails. Slugs of the family Testacillidae are large (6–12 cm long when extended), have a small shell at the rear that covers the lung and are carnivorous, feeding on earthworms. All slugs and snails have unsegmented bodies with four tentacles on their heads, the upper pair being larger with eyespots at the tip. All molluscs are most active in moist conditions; during periods of dry, windy weather they seek shelter and become inactive above ground. A decrease in light intensity, together with a fall in temperature and rise in humidity encourage the animals to venture out on to vegetation. They feed on a wide range of living and decaying plant material and damage appears as irregular holes with smooth edges caused by the rasping action of their mouth-parts. Plant seedlings and young plants can be chewed and killed while older plants may be severely damaged. A slime trail is nearly always present and may lead to the pest's resting-place. Mature slugs and snails are hermaphroditic, having both female and male reproductive organs. When mating, mature animals slide against each other and both adults may be fertilized simultaneously. Clusters of eggs are laid in soil or decaying organic matter, which provides the necessary protection from adverse conditions (freezing and desiccation). Some species may have two or more generations per year while others living in cooler environments may take a couple of years to mature.

Natural enemies of slugs and snails include insectivorous mammals (hedgehogs and moles), several birds, frogs, toads and lizards, parasitic flies (Sciomyzidae), predatory insects such as carabid beetles and entomopathogenic nematodes such as *Phasmarhabditis hermaphrodita*.

70 *Cepaea hortensis* (Müller) (white-lipped banded snail) on a damaged hosta leaf.

71 *Helix aspersa* (Müller) (garden snail) on lettuce leaves.

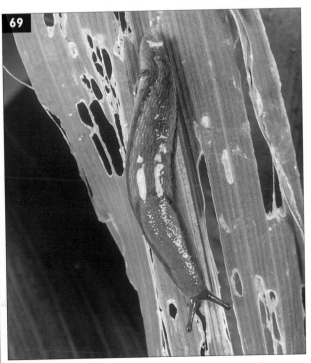

69 *Arion distinctus* slug on a severely damaged maize leaf.

WOODLICE
ISOPODA (72–75)

Woodlice, pillbugs, slaters or sowbugs are all common names for the group of insect related organisms that are actually crustaceans, making them closer to crabs, crayfish and shrimp. Some woodlice are brown with small spots, slaters tend to be a uniform slate-grey but other species may be more colourful including a few which are a rose-pink colour. Adult sizes range from about 2.5 mm up to 18 mm in length. They all live in damp habitats such as under decaying wood and plant matter, stones and rocks with a degree of moist organic matter interspaced such as in a rockery. Indeed a moist environment is required for their survival, as they will quickly die if exposed to warm dry air. Although regarded as pests when they feed on seedlings, fruit and mushrooms their omnivorous diet allows them to feed on dead plants, animal remains, fungi and dung, thus performing a valuable role in recycling nutrients. On many plants damage resembles slug feeding but without the characteristic slime trail; old-feeding areas may become heavily scarred with elongated calluses.

The feeding site depends on pest species, some feed below soil level (*Porcellio* spp.), others girdle the base of stems (*Armadillidium* spp.) while some that eat fruit and leaves may be found well away from the ground, particularly in very humid environments (*Oniscus* spp.).

The segmented body has a clearly defined head region with a pair of compound eyes, two pairs of antennae (one pair are minute and hardly discernible), a pair of mandibles armed with teeth and small jointed appendages used in the manipulation of food. The seven-segmented thoracic region makes up the majority of the body and carries a pair of simple, jointed legs on each segment. A narrow six-segmented abdomen often ends in a tail and in some species the abdomen forms a cavity containing a moisture rich pouch within which air tubules can 'breath' rather like a gill. Gravid females have a brood pouch formed by pairs of overlapping plates growing from the legs of thoracic segments 2–5; depending on species up to 200 eggs (commonly 20–50) may be carried in the pouch for up to 1 month before hatching. Hatchlings are white, about 1 mm in length and remain in the brood pouch for a week or so before dispersing. They attain their adult colouration after about a fortnight and moult several times before reaching adulthood.

The principal natural enemies of woodlice include centipedes, particularly lithobiids that will kill many young woodlice. Several ground beetles including staphelinids and carabids are recorded as feeding on woodlice. Parasitoid wasps, often specific to certain species of woodlice, can be found worldwide. Spiders of the Clubionid and Dyseridae families are reported to include woodlice in their diet. Other predators of woodlice include birds, reptiles and mammals. Probably the easiest way of controlling or reducing woodlice is to remove additional sources of food, all hiding places and dry the area as much as possible.

73 A small woodlouse with an unusual pink colour.

74 *Oniscus asellus* (Linnaeus) (woodlouse).

72 Adult and immature woodlice over-wintering under a brick.

75 *Armadillidium vulgare* (pill bug).

SECTION 3:
BENEFICIAL ARTHROPOD PROFILES

- COLEOPTERA
- CARABIDAE
- STAPHYLINIDAE
- CICINDELIDAE
- DERMAPTERA
- DIPTERA
- CECIDOMYIIDAE
- SYRPHIDAE

- HETEROPTERA
- HYMENOPTERA
- NEUROPTERA
- ARACHNIDAE
- OPILIONES
- ACARI
- CHILOPODA

This section will profile many of the terrestrial parasitoid and predatory arthropods found in a wide range of cropping situations. A parasitoid is an organism that feeds in or on another animal during some portion of its life cycle, consuming all or most of prey body tissues. In this symbiotic relationship the parasitoid provides no benefit to the host, which may be killed or at least drastically weakened, and be unable to reproduce. Several parasitoid wasps are specific in what host and even at what stage of the host they attack and can therefore have a narrow window of opportunity in which to reproduce. Solitary species deposit one egg per host, e.g. *Aphidius* spp. and *Encarsia* spp., while gregarious species can produce several parasitoids from each host, e.g. *Cotesia glomerata*.

Predators tend to be less specialized in their food requirements, many being polyphagous between families and life stages of suitable prey organisms, e.g. *Chrysoperla* spp. Most predators do not need to synchronize with their prey; providing sufficient prey is present in the immediate area they will continue to develop and reproduce. Many predators are carnivorous as both adult and nymph (e.g. *Macrolophus* spp.). While many of the ground beetles are predatory as adults the Neuroptera and Syrphidae have only predatory larvae.

One common, although arbitrary factor, is that this group of organisms are all visible to the naked eye at the adult and usually the larval or nymphal stage (many parasitoids develop within a host and must be dissected to be observed). The final section of this book deals with examples of entomopathogens or microbiologicals that frequently require some magnification.

Coleoptera

Beetles are recognizable by the hard or leathery forewings (elytra) that often completely cover the more delicate and membranous hindwings. Several species do not possess any hindwings and are thus incapable of flight; however, in all instances there is a fine line along the dorsal surface marking where the two wing cases join. This is in contrast to the Hemiptera where the wings are folded over the body, often displaying a membranous wing tip. All beetles have biting mouth-parts and are able to penetrate the outer skin of most insects and mites. Beetles are typically active hunters with both adults and larvae showing rapid movement. Larvae similarly have biting jaws very much like the adult and frequently eat the same type of food. The larvae of most species have six legs situated in pairs on the first three thoracic segments but, unlike caterpillars, beetle larvae have no prolegs on the abdomen. They may pupate in close proximity to their main food source; some species produce a simple pupal case on the ground and in most instances they are most vulnerable to predation by other organisms while in the pupal stage.

FAMILY: COCCINELLIDAE
(LADYBIRD BEETLES) (76–80)

Adult coccinellid or ladybird beetles range from 0.8–18 mm in length and have an oval body with a convex dorsal surface and a flat ventral surface and biting mouth-parts. Coccinellid adults have fully developed hindwings and many species fly readily. There is considerable colour variation within species and there are several distinct recognized forms of many of the commoner species. When disturbed many species fall through vegetation like half a ball-bearing and disappear from view in leaf litter.

Most commonly known coccinellids are predators of aphids in gardens as well as orchards and arable crops. However, other species attack scale insects, mites, mealybugs and whitefly. Some Coccinellidae are fungivores.

Coccinellids can be encouraged into agricultural crops by provision of sources of suitable prey in the margins or beneath trees at a time when the crop pest is not present. For example, while many aphids are plant specific and will not attack a neighbouring crop plant, many of the coccinellid species will attack aphids on plants in the margin and then move into a cropped area if aphids arrive. Proximity of suitable hibernation sites such as grassy banks, hedgerows or woodland can have a profound influence on the abundance of coccinellids in agricultural areas.

76 *Coccinella septempunctata* adult feeding on *Aphis fabae* (black bean aphids).

77 *Mysia oblongoguttata* (Linnaeus) ladybird feeding on *Aphis fabae* (black bean aphid).

78 *Anatis ocellata* (Linnaeus) (eyed ladybird) (photograph courtesy of Peter Wilson/Holt Studios).

79 Vegetarian *Thea 22-punctata* (Linnaeus)(22-spot ladybird) adult.

80 *Coccinella magnifica* (scarce 7-spot ladybird) associated with wood ant nests.

ADALIA BIPUNCTATA (LINNAEUS) (2-SPOT LADYBIRD) (81–83)

Species characteristics

The legs and underside of the abdomen of *Adalia bipunctata* are black, markings on elytra are variable but usually a single black mark is present centrally on each hindwing (elytron). Elytra can be almost black with a few red marks. *A. bipunctata* can exhibit at least 12 recognized forms, with varying amounts of red and black. One of the most familiar ladybirds it is 4–5 mm in length, and is often found feeding on aphids on trees and shrubs but also on vegetables such as broad beans, feeding on the black bean aphid *Aphis fabae* (Scopoli). *A. bipunctata* occurs on this plant (as tic beans) in arable fields but is not common in other arable crops such as cereals. It is diurnal and plant-active, although adults and larvae are found on the ground in late summer when aphid populations are sparse.

Life cycle

A. bipunctata over-winters in groups, sometimes large, in buildings, under bark and is sometimes discovered in larders among neglected cereal packets. In spring, adults emerging from hibernation in the cooler parts of houses find their way to windows. The adults mate in spring, and lay their yellow eggs in batches of 5–50 or more, stacked end on, usually to the lower surface of leaves. Batches on brassica plants are likely to be those of the large white butterfly *Artogeia* (*Pieris*) *brassicae* (Linnaeus). Larvae are slate-grey with orange markings, and when nearly fully grown are more voracious than the adults. Cannibalism occurs if aphid populations 'crash' before the ladybirds have completed development. They hold onto the leaf with an anal sucker, especially when feeding or pupating. Pupae are black and are found on leaves and stems.

Crop/pest associations

A. bipunctata is common as an aphid predator of garden broad beans, and on elder (*Sambucus nigra*), although the aphid on this shrub is rather toxic to them. Black bean aphid is also a sub-optimal prey. On trees, it is a common predator of aphids on lime (*Tilia* spp.) and sycamore (*Acer* spp.), where it may not reduce bean aphid populations but can accelerate declines, leading to fewer aphids to lay over-wintering eggs.

Influence on growing practices

A. bipunctata benefits from pollen sources in the spring and from other field-margin resources such as non-pest aphids on plants such as nettles (*Urtica dioica*). It has a low aphid density threshold for egg laying, but may not appear in fields early enough or in high enough numbers to reduce black bean aphid populations. The slight toxicity of the aphids may be another factor, and proximity of over-wintering sites may also affect the numbers entering fields and gardens in the spring.

81 *Adalia bipunctata* adults, two colour variations feeding on *Macrosiphum rosae* (rose aphids).

82 *A. bipunctata* adults, two colour variations feeding on rosy *Dysaphis plantaginea* (rosy apple aphids).

83 Another colour variant *of A. bipunctata* adult.

CHILOCORUS BIPUSTULATUS (LINNAEUS) (84–86)

Species characteristics

Adults and larvae of *Chilocorus bipustulatus* are predators of scale insects in fruit and citrus crops in Europe. *C. hexacyclus*, *C. stigma* and *C. tricyphus* are found in a similar role in North America. Adult *C. bipustulatus* are small (3.3–4.5 mm in length) with a very shiny convex black body and characteristic red spots looking like an exclamation mark in the centre of each wing case.

Life cycle

Eggs are oval, 1–2 mm long, yellow to orange in colour and are laid singly in association with scale insect prey. Larvae are covered in spines and tubercles and increase in size from 1 mm to 7 mm in length. *Chilocorus* spp. normally have three to four generations per year in Mediterranean regions and two generations further north. In late summer, typically early autumn in southern France, adult *Chilocorus* spp. leave the orchards and fly to overwintering sites.

Crop/pest associations

Chilocorus spp. are important predators of scales in apples, primarily *Lepidosaphes ulmi*, *Epidiaspis leperii* and *Quadraspidiotus perniciosus*. Individuals typically consume 20–40 scale insects per day.

Influence on growing practices

Like most Coccinellidae the eggs, larvae and adults of *Chilocorus* spp. are very susceptible to insecticides. This may be enhanced by the fact that they consume their prey rather than sucking out the body contents, as does a mirid or anthocorid bug. Unfortunately, their scale insect prey are protected by waxy secretions and are much less susceptible to pesticide sprays.

84 *Chilocoris* sp. larva.

85 *Chilocoris* sp. pupa.

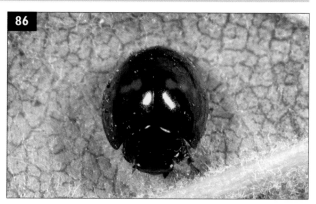

86 *Chilocoris* sp. adult.

COCCINELLA SEPTEMPUNCTATA (LINNAEUS) (7-SPOT LADYBIRD) (87–96)

Species characteristics

Coccinella septempunctata are 5.5 mm in length or larger, and nearly always have three black spots on each red elytron, with one central spot behind the thorax. It is found in gardens and arable fields but rarely on shrubs and trees, usually on low vegetation. Pale elytra mean a newly emerged adult, or sometimes a parasitoid within.

Life cycle

C. septempunctata over-winters singly or in small groups, in curled leaves of plants such as box, dry vegetation in gardens and hedge bases, and occasionally in clusters on the lower branches and stems of low-growing shrubs. There is usually one generation per year in arable land and it is the most frequent ladybird species in wheat. Larval densities in mid summer may exceed 100/m². Larvae are commonly found on the soil at this time, moving rapidly on hot days, as aphid populations disappear due to crop ripening. *C. septempunctata* is often attacked by the parasitoid wasp *Perilitus coccinellae*, and at the end of winter 60–70% of dispersing adults may be parasitized. The parasitoid's cocoon is spun between the legs of the adult ladybird which eventually dies, though not immediately following the parasitoid's emergence. The beetle is paralysed and dies of starvation or fungal attack, its fat reserves having been consumed by the parasitoid's larva.

Crop/pest associations

C. septempunctata is common in gardens and especially in cereal fields if aphids are abundant. Late summer swarms, which sometimes are numerous enough to appear in TV and newspaper reports, probably come from ripening wheat fields following outbreaks of grain aphid *Sitobion avenae* (Linnaeus).

Influence on growing practices

Insecticide use on wheat in summer probably kills millions of these insects; if larvae are in the crop, they are either killed by the spray or starve to death when their aphid prey are killed. Herbicides used to 'clean up' hedge bases destroy perennial grasses, leaving annual vegetation with a shallower layer of dead and dying vegetation to provide refuges in winter. Over-tidy gardens are also inimical to this species' chances of surviving the winter for the same reason.

87 *Coccinella* sp. eggs.

88 *Coccinella* sp. young larvae.

89 *Coccinella* sp. young larva and eggs.

90 *Coccinella septempunctata* larva feeding on *Aphis fabae*.

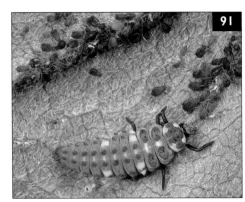

91 *C. septempunctata* larva feeding on *A. fabae*.

92 *C. septempunctata* pupa.

93 *C. septempunctata* adult newly emerged with colouration and spots developing.

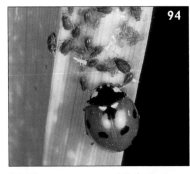

94 *C. septempunctata* adult feeding on *Rhopalosiphum padi* (bird-cherry aphids).

95 *C. septempunctata* adult feeding on *Aphis pomi* (apple aphids).

96 *C. septempunctata* adults hibernating (photograph courtesy of Phil McLean/Holt Studios).

CRYPTOLAEMUS MONTROUZIERI (MULSANT) (97–99)

Species characteristics

The mealybug predator *Cryptolaemus montrouzieri* originated from Australia via California, to reach most areas of the world and control a wide range of mealybugs. The adult ladybird-shaped beetle belongs to the family Coccinellidae. It is about 4 mm in length, has dark brown/black wing covers and orange head, prothorax, wing tips and abdomen. Larvae are covered in mealy wax-like projections making them (particularly the young larvae) resemble their host mealybug, and can reach up to 13 mm in length. All stages of *C. montrouzieri* are predatory, with adults and young larvae preferring host eggs and young nymphs, while older larvae will consume all stages of mealybug.

Life cycle

Females mate soon after emergence and start egg laying about five days later; between 200 and 700 eggs are laid singly into mealybug egg masses. The number of eggs produced depends strongly on the adult females' diet, and starvation can halt egg production. Several hundred mealybugs may be eaten during development of the predator.

Crop/pest associations

Larvae move freely over plants in search of prey, and in periods of shortage can become cannibalistic. Adults under similar conditions fly off in search of more prey. *C. montrouzieri* are also polyphagous, feeding on aphids and scale insects when necessary. They can over-winter in glasshouses but generally fresh insects are introduced for control each spring.

Influence on growing practices

Temperature can have a marked effect on the development of *C. montrouzieri*, which takes about 25 days at 30°C (86°F) and up to 72 days at 18°C (64°F), there being no activity at below 9°C (48°F). Sunshine also plays an important part by making the insect much more active. The eggs of *C. montrouzieri* are well protected from pesticides in the mealybug egg masses. However, the larvae and adults are reasonably tolerant to most short persistence pesticides.

97 *Cryptolaemus montrouzieri* larva.

98 *C. montrouzieri* adults with *Planococcus citri* (citrus mealybug).

99 *C. montrouzieri* adult feeding on *P. citri*.

DELPHASTUS CATALINAE (HORN) (100)

Species characteristics

Adult *Delphastus catalinae* are small, shiny black beetles 1.3–1.4 mm in length, and are related to the aphid feeding ladybirds (Coccinellidae). However, this predator devours large numbers of whitefly, with both adults and larvae consuming all stages of their host. The pale yellowish-white larvae are relatively immobile and can starve if their food source runs out before they reach pupation. *D. catalinae* is distributed widely across central and southern USA, south through central and South America as far as Peru. Their use in the UK and parts of Europe requires ministerial license, which is usually granted on the basis of non-survival outside the protected environment of a glasshouse.

Life cycle

Adults require 50–100 whitefly eggs/cm^2 before oviposition can commence. This high level of whitefly helps survival of the offspring. Egg to adult development is 21 days at 28.3°C (82°F) which is approximately three days slower than the host at similar temperatures. Adult and larvae feed predominately on young whitefly nymphs. The average longevity is 60–65 days; however, diet plays an important role as adults can live for up to 80 days feeding on pest larvae, which is significantly longer than males or females feeding on eggs alone.

Crop/pest associations

There is much interest in this predator for suppression of potentially out of control or rapidly breeding whitefly populations, particularly against *Bemisia tabaci* and *Trialeurodes*

101 *Harmonia conglobata* adult with pink spotted colour variation feeding on aphids.

100 *Delphastus* sp. feeding on *Trialeurodes vaporariorum* (glasshouse whitefly) scales.

102 *H. conglobata* adult with red spots on a black ground colour variation feeding on aphids.

vaporiorum on protected crops. *D. catalinae* is commercially used for control of whitefly, particularly in localized 'hot spots' as frequently occur in amateur glasshouses, where pest numbers can increase to levels uncontrollable by the normal parasitoids. This often happens when wide ranges of individual plants are kept and the various susceptibilities of plants allow small populations of a pest to build up to damaging levels. As a first line of defence, routine introductions of parasitoids are suggested with the use of *D. catalinae* as a backup control.

Influence on growing practices

Use of *D. catalinae* in combination with whitefly parasitoids has shown that whitefly containing eggs and immature larvae are at risk of predation, but as the parasitoid larvae develops and pupates the risk is greatly reduced. This is probably due to a hardening of the whitefly cuticle when the parasitoid pupates, making it unpalatable for the predator. The term 'biological pesticide' has been coined for this voracious predator, which invariably eats many prey but rarely establishes itself in the glasshouse.

103 *H. conglobata* adults with three colour variations including unspotted.

HARMONIA CONGLOBATA (LINNAEUS) (101–103)

Species characteristics

Harmonia conglobata is an aphid predator in fruit crops, particularly in southern Europe. Adults are large (3.4–5 mm in length) and are recognized by the elytra which are coloured pale pink with eight black angular spots. Larvae are grey with pink dorsal spots.

Life cycle

H. conglobata is multivoltine and can produce three or four generations a year in a Mediterranean climate, falling to two generations per year in a temperate climate. In early autumn adults leave the orchards and fly to aggregate at over-wintering sites, often in prominent locations overlooking the orchards.

Crop/pest associations

Adults and larvae are voracious predators of aphids, particularly *Aphis pomi* and *Dysaphis plantaginea* in apple orchards, *Myzus cerasi* in cherries, and *Myzus persicae* in peaches. *H. conglobata* develops and breeds equally well when feeding on

either *A. pomi* or *D. plantaginea*. More offspring are produced if adults feed on *M. persicae* or *M. cerasi*. Coccinellids alone seem unable to prevent the summer explosion of *A. pomi*, which occurs when some species (e.g. *Adalia bipunctata*) are in summer diapause and which reaches a peak when *H. conglobata* becomes less active. It is also possible that in mid summer *A. pomi* becomes less palatable to ladybirds.

Influence on growing practices

Aphidophagous ladybirds are without exception sensitive to insecticides and will be killed by most treatments made to control aphids. However, *H. conglobata* may occur in margins and on trees surrounding an orchard. Care to avoid spray drift and treatment of non-target habitats would reduce the risk to these predators.

HIPPODAMIA CONVERGENS (GUERIN-MENEVILLE) (104, 105)

Species characteristics

Hippodamia convergens is a highly voracious predator, capable of eating 50–60 aphids daily; it can also feed on numerous other insect or mite prey. Adults of this ladybird or lady beetle can vary in size up to 7 mm in length and can have up to 13 black spots on their red elytra. However, they all have a set of white lines that converge behind the head, giving the common name convergent lady beetle.

Life cycle

Each female can produce up to 1000 eggs at a rate of 10–50 per day over a 1–3 month period. These are usually deposited in small clusters close to their prey and may be found on leaves or stems. The eggs are about 1 mm long, yellow to orange colour and spindle shaped. They hatch after 2–5 days to tiny alligator-like larvae, which begin feeding almost immediately on their own egg cases followed by insect or mite prey. Depending on food availability and temperature, the larvae can grow to between 5 and 7 mm in length over a 12–30 day period, travelling up to 12 m in search of prey. When fully developed the larva attaches itself by the abdomen to a leaf, stem, string or other firm surface to pupate. This stage may last from 3–14 days depending on temperature before the adult emerges.

Crop/pest associations

H. convergens is the most abundant *Hippodamia* species in North America and is now widespread throughout most of the world. It was successfully introduced to Chile from California in 1903 to control scale insects. It has recently become available in several European countries, but is prohibited in the UK which does not allow releases of wild harvested organisms. Each generation (larva and adult) of *H. convergens* is capable of killing up to 5000 aphids. They can also feed on many other soft-bodied insects, mites and their eggs, including adelgids, beetle larvae, psyllids, mealybugs, scale insects, spider mites, thrips and whitefly. Ladybirds are susceptible to fungal attack and parasitism, which can reduce their numbers later in the season.

Influence on growing practices

Such active predators tend to eliminate a pest population quite rapidly and find themselves with insufficient food to maintain a constant presence, particularly on protected crops. In field or garden situations they tend to survive better by feeding on a wider diet and having a better distribution. Currently *Hippodamia* spp. are collected from wild populations by vacuuming over-wintering beetles from aggregation sites (under tree bark and also specially placed shelters). Introduced *H. convergens* (and some other ladybird species) have become a problem in North America where they have competed with indigenous coccinellid species; they also bite humans when starved. These 'harvested' insects need to be fed and conditioned to be ready for use, otherwise they are likely to fly off in a spring migratory flight before any eggs are laid on the crops to be protected.

104 *Hippodamia convergens* adult feeding on *Rhopalosiphum padi* (bird-cherry aphids).

105 *H. convergens* adult feeding on *Aphis pomi* (apple aphid) but confronted by a red ant *Messor* sp.

PROPYLEA 14-PUNCTATA (LINNAEUS) (14-SPOT LADYBIRD) (106–108)

Species characteristics

Propylea 14-punctata has yellow elytra with more or less square shaped black marks, usually seven on each elytron but often fused so it is difficult to differentiate 14 clear spots. The pronotum (main part of the dorsal surface of the thorax) has an irregular, single black mark. Legs are orange-yellow and the lower surface is mainly black. The larva has brighter yellow markings than does that of a similar-sized 2-spot ladybird.

Life cycle

P. 14-punctata is a typical ladybird of temperate Europe, with over-wintering adults giving rise to one summer generation. The winter adults are not found in large numbers, unlike the aggregations of the 2-spot. It is diurnal and a plant-active species and occurs especially on low-growing plants. *P. 14-punctata* is rarely as abundant as 2-spots and 7-spots.

Crop/pest associations

P. 14-punctata is most easily found in arable crops; it can be as abundant as 7-spots but is usually second in importance to this species in terms of biological control of aphids, e.g. in cereals. Enormous swarms of ladybirds occur in late summer, following a mild winter and a hot summer (leading to high aphid populations in cereals), and will include this species but the 7-spot dominates. Winter wheat is the crop most likely to harbour *P. 14-punctata*, although it does occur in gardens.

Influence on growing practices

Although *P. 14-punctata* can be abundant in arable crops and probably contributes usefully to the reduction in aphid populations, it is under-studied; little is known of its over-wintering needs, or indeed of where it spends most of the year outside the 6–8 week aphid season in cereals. Insecticide use and mis-managed field boundaries are likely to be inimical to this predator, but detailed studies on its ecology have not been carried out.

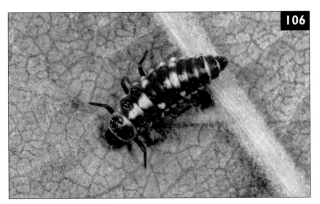

106 *Propylea 14-punctata* larva.

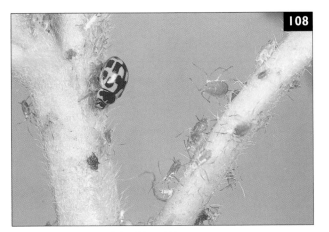

107 *P. 14-punctata* adult.

108 *P. 14-punctata* adult with aphids.

SCYMNUS SUBVILLOSUS (GOEZE) (109, 110)

Species characteristics

Adults of *Scymnus subvillosus* are small (2.0–2.5 mm long), mostly black, with elliptical bronze coloured spots at the front of each wing case and with a covering of fine hairs. Larvae are covered in tubercles with white waxy secretions.

Life cycle

S. subvillosus has two to four generations per year depending on climatic conditions.

Crop/pest associations

Scymnus spp. are minor predators of both aphids and spider mites in apple and pear orchards. They can feed on low populations of aphids such as *Aphis pomi* and tend to be found in higher numbers at the time when aphid numbers are falling. One adult *S. subvillosus* consumes approximately eight aphids per day.

Influence on growing practices

Adults and larvae are susceptible to insecticides, both directly and through consuming treated prey.

109 *Scymnus subvillosus* larva (photograph courtesy of Len McLeod/Holt Studios).

110 *Scymnus frontalis* (Fabricius) adult (photograph courtesy of Frank Koehler [Bornheim, Germany]).

STETHORUS PUNCTILLUM (WEISE) (111–113)

Species characteristics

Adult *Stethorus punctillum* are small (1.0–1.5 mm long), black ladybirds, hemispherical in shape with fine yellow hairs covering the elytra. Larvae are dark brown to black and up to 2.5 mm in length with setae on the sides of each segment. Both adults and larvae are predators of *Panonychus ulmi* (Koch) (fruit tree red spider mite) on fruit trees in northern and southern Europe. *S. punctillum* can also be found in hedgerows and woodland where it preys upon other species of spider mites

Life cycle

S. punctillum over-winters as an adult in crevices and under the bark of trees, usually emerging in late spring. Eggs are laid on the underside of leaves or occasionally on twigs in early summer, in close proximity to spider mites. Eggs are oval and pale cream coloured. In northern Europe a second generation lays eggs in late summer. In southern Europe there may be as many as four generations in one year. The development from egg to adult takes approximately 24 days. Adults generally hibernate in autumn on dried leaves either on the tree or on the soil.

Crop/pest associations

In fruit orchards *S. punctillum* feeds entirely on mites, preferring to consume adult prey. Adults feed spasmodically and consume on average 20 mites per day. Larvae consume on average 24 mites a day. In the autumn the winter eggs of spider mites are eaten by adults and larvae of *S. punctillum*.

Influence on growing practices

All stages of *S. punctillum* are susceptible to insecticides. Winter washes with tar oils in the 1950s harmed over-wintering adults and were thought to have contributed to the emergence of *P. ulmi* as a pest species.

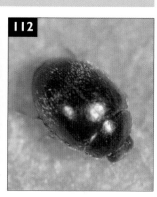

111 *Stethorus punctillum* larva.   112 *S. punctillum* adult.

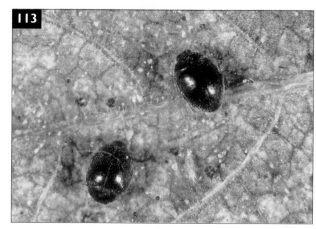

113 *S. punctillum* adults feeding on spider mites.

Carabidae

ORDER: COLEOPTERA
FAMILY: CARABIDAE
GROUND BEETLES

Many ground beetles of the family Carabidae are active polyphagous predators as both larvae and adults in almost all crops and gardens (**114–122**). Carabids can be found under stones and in damp places in the daytime, and many are active as predators only at night. Whilst the larvae are almost entirely predatory the adults of most species consume a mixture of plant and animal food. Some genera, such as *Harpalus* and *Amara* are largely seed feeders and climb plants in search of food. Carabids are entirely terrestrial beetles and the adults can be recognized by their relatively long legs (adapted for running) and by their filiform (threadlike) antennae. The wing cases cover the abdomen in most species but only a few genera fly readily. Different carabid species are found in different habitat types, with moisture and soil type being strong determining factors.

114 Head and thorax of an attractive but extremely rare ground beetle *Carabus intricatus* (Linnaeus).

115 Ground beetles sheltering under a stone.

120 *Carabus monilis* (Fabricius).

116–118 Three examples of ground beetle larvae.

121 *Carabus nemoralis* (Müller).

119 *Carabus granulatus* (Linnaeus).

122 *Nebria complanata* (Linnaeus).

AGONUM DORSALE (PONTOPPIDAN) (123, 124)

Species characteristics
Agonum dorsale is a medium-sized (6–8 mm), fast-running beetle with a small, narrow pronotum and long, slender, pale brown legs. Elytra are bi-coloured, with browny-orange background and a large blue metallic patch towards the base. It is nocturnal, occasionally plant-active, but mainly ground-based. Population density is rather variable between years.

Life cycle
A. dorsale hibernate as adults in grassy tussocks, under stones, often in field margins. It may be found in very dense aggregations in sheltered areas in gardens. *A. dorsale* is very active in early spring, moving into fields and laying eggs. Larvae are probably subterranean, with the next generation of adults returning to over-wintering sites in the early autumn. Peak abundance in fields occurs in early summer. Adults are winged.

Crop/pest associations
These predators are voracious consumers of small, invertebrate prey, including aphids that have fallen to the ground or that are on accessible plant parts. A large proportion of individuals contain aphids in their guts in the early summer, and populations can aggregate in areas of high aphid density.

Influence on growing practices
A. dorsale is protected from normal winter cultivations and flooding by hibernation away from open ground. It may be affected by spring applications of pesticides that harm over-wintering adults as they enter the field. However, this is one of the carabid species that seems to live in cultivated areas, and there is evidence that populations go extinct when cultivation ceases.

BEMBIDION LAMPROS (LATREILLE) (125, 126)

Species characteristics
Bembidion lampros is a small (3–4 mm), metallic, bronzy-black beetle with slender legs. The most important diagnostic character is the rudimentary maxillary palp, only visible under magnification. It is part of a large genus and is widely distributed in cultivated habitats as a day-active, ground-based predator. It is rarely found in dry or sandy soils.

Life cycle
Adults over-winter in hedgerows and grassy tussocks, emerging in the early spring to lay eggs in open crop habitats. Larvae are rarely seen and the new generation of adults emerge from mid summer onwards, returning to the hedgerow in early autumn. *B. lampros* is known to aestivate in hotter, dryer conditions in the field in mid summer.

Crop pest associations
Adults are active soil invertebrate feeders, including aphids, carrot fly eggs and springtails. They are particularly active in vegetable crops and are ranked highly as an early spring predator, active before other species appear.

Influence on growing practices
Populations can be rather variable between years; however, presence in field boundaries and spring breeding may ensure rapid exploitation of the crop by *B. lampros*, as long as the adults that have over-wintered are not affected by pesticides applied in the spring.

125 *Bembidion lampros* attacking an aphid.

123 *Agonum dorsale* adult.

126 *B. lampros* beetles competing for an aphid.

124 *A. dorsale* adult.

CARABUS VIOLACEUS (LINNAEUS) (127, 128)

Species characteristics
Carabus violaceus is a large (24–29 mm) black ground beetle with a blue to purple metallic sheen at the margin of the elytra and with a bluish tinge to the edges of the pronotum. The elytra have very fine striation compared with other species of the genus giving them a matt appearance. Other species of this genus, e.g. *C. granulatus* (**119**), *C. monilis* (**120**) and *C. nemoralis* (**121**) typically have granulations and characteristic patterns in their elytral sculpture. Like most others of the genus this species is nocturnal but may be found in the daytime under stones or in dense vegetation. Since the adults can inflict a painful bite and can release irritant substances from their anal glands it is best to avoid handling them.

Life cycle
C. violaceus breeds from mid summer to autumn. Eggs are 5 mm × 0.5 mm and are laid singly in soil. Larval development takes from 60–80 days. The beetle over-winters as a larva. Adults emerge and are active from spring to early autumn and are active on the surface.

Crop pest associations
Carabus is mainly a Palearctic genus with only a few species occurring in North America or in the Oriental region. *C. violaceus* is found in Britain and eastern Europe but, with the exception of the Vosges, is not found in France. This beetle is known to consume slugs, snails, earthworms and insects in both gardens and agricultural fields.

Influence on growing practices
In northern Europe *C. violaceus* is considered to be a forest species yet is also commonly found in gardens and in agricultural fields, particularly grass and arable crops once there is a canopy to retain humidity. Large carabids prefer moist habitats and are unlikely to be found in large dry fields with few refugia. Relatively few individuals of this genus are collected in field samples so the effects of crop protection products on them are rarely evaluated in studies.

DEMETRIAS ATRICAPILLUS (LINNAEUS) (129, 130)

Species characteristics
Demetrias atricapillus has a long narrow pronotum, with the head the same breadth. The body is yellowish-red and the head is black. It is diurnal and plant-active, adhesive tarsi permitting adults to climb cereal and grass stems in search of prey. *D. atricapillus* is very common, especially on grasses and nettles, and is very widely distributed in a variety of crop habitats; it is sometimes found in piles of garden refuse. Some *Demetrias* species are associated with water.

Life cycle
Adults over-winter in grassy tussocks, especially *Dactylis* and *Holcus* species in the boundaries of agricultural fields. They become active in the early spring and migrate into the open crop, climbing foliage of the growing plants. They may migrate up to 100 m. The larvae are rarely seen, are possibly subterranean, and pupation takes place in the soil with the next generation of adults migrating back to over-wintering sites in the late summer.

Crop/pest associations
D. atricapillus is active early in the spring as over-wintered adults that forage to build up energy reserves for egg laying. It is best known in cereal crops, where this species seems to specialize in consuming aphids. Early season aphid predation may be important in preventing later outbreaks; species such as this that over-winter in the field boundary are consuming aphids months before predators like ladybirds colonize crops.

Influence on growing practices
Being diurnal and plant active, *D. atricapillus* is exposed to direct spraying by pesticides. It seems however, to be amongst the most tolerant of all invertebrates to some pesticides, especially synthetic pyrethroids. The most important factor influencing its density in fields is the quality and the proximity of over-wintering habitats to the field. Some farmers introduce raised, grassy banks to the centres of fields to ensure that predators such as *D. atricapillus* penetrate the whole crop at an early stage in the spring.

127 *Carabus violaceus* attacking a slug.

129 *Demetrias atricapillus* feeding on an aphid.

128 *C. violaceus* attacking a slug.

130 *D. atricapillus* feeding on an aphid.

131 *Harpalus rufipes* adult plant-active ground beetle.

132 *H. rufipes* attacking a slug.

133 *Loricera pilicornis* adult beetle.

134 *L. pilicornis* adult beetle's characteristic antennae.

HARPALUS RUFIPES (DE GEER) (131, 132)

Species characteristics
Harpalus rufipes is a large (10–17 mm), stout-bodied beetle with short legs. Elytra are covered in a dense, yellowish, velvety pubescence. Legs may be pale to dark brown but the head and pronotum are black. A very common species, it is associated with relatively dry areas. Nocturnally active, it is known to climb wheat and other crop plants and feed from aphid colonies.

Life cycle
Both larvae and adults may over-winter deep in the soil, with spring and late summer breeding phases the next year. Most commonly, adults from over-wintered larvae are active in the late summer and breeding may continue into a second year. Larvae are weed seed feeders. Adults are winged and are one of the few carabids to be seen flying on warm summer days.

Crop/pest associations
H. rufipes is commonly found in cereal fields and may consume aphids on the ground or on plants. Adults may also feed on strawberry seeds, but rarely constitute pests, and on molluscs.

Influence on growing practices
H. rufipes is relatively protected from sprays when hibernating underground and may rapidly colonize habitats by flight. Population recovery after toxic sprays may be rapid. *H. rufipes* tends to be numerous every year.

LORICERA PILICORNIS (FABRICIUS) (133, 134)

Species characteristics
Loricera pilicornis is a relatively small (6–8 mm), black beetle with protruding eyes. The first six segments of the antennae are bristled. The elytra each bear three, round depressions. A relatively common, ground-active predator, it is associated with damper field and garden habitats.

Life cycle
Winged adults may over-winter in wooded areas and hedgerows, but enter fields in the spring. Larvae appear in the spring and are surface-active, pupation takes place in the soil. The next generation of adults emerges mid to late summer and migrates from open fields in the late summer and early autumn.

Crop/pest associations
L. pilicornis is an active predator of small invertebrates, including springtails and aphids that are walking on the soil surface. Early spring activity of egg-laying adults may contribute to pest suppression before other predators arrive.

Influence on growing practices
Insecticide application in the spring may suppress over-wintering adults or early stage larvae, reducing population size in the next generation. This is one of the ground beetle species that survives best in disturbed or cultivated land and is locally extinct in areas where cultivation has ceased.

NEBRIA BREVICOLLIS (FABRICIUS) (135–137)

Species characteristics

Nebria brevicollis is a large (10–13 mm), brown to black beetle, with long, slender legs. The antennae and terminal limb segments may be reddish brown and the pronotum is relatively short. It is a very common field and garden predator associated with damper cultivated areas. *N. brevicollis* scuttles over the soil surface when disturbed by cultivations in the autumn.

Life cycle

After summer diapause, adults lay eggs in the soil. Larvae are surface active in the autumn and winter and both are well known to gardeners. Very few adults survive to the end of the winter and the larvae constitute the main over-wintering population. This species is thought to have originated from woodland and has a strong association with field margins and hedgerows. The adults are winged, but are rarely seen flying.

Crop/pest associations

N. brevicollis is a voracious predator of aphids and other invertebrate prey on the ground, including molluscs. It is one of the rare, winter-active predators and is very common in gardens.

Influence on growing practices

N. brevicollis is affected by autumn/winter spray applications before crop canopy protects the soil from receiving a full dose of insecticide. Both larvae and adults may be adversely affected and large population reductions are frequent. Populations are variable between years, partly as a result of this. It is also sensitive to some of the chemicals in slug pellets. This is, however, a species that thrives in association with cultivation, populations going extinct when cultivation ceases.

135 *Nebria brevicollis* adult beetle.

136 *N. brevicollis* adult beetles.

137 *N. brevicollis* close-up of mouth-parts.

NOTIOPHILUS BIGUTTATUS (FABRICIUS) (138)

Species characteristics
Notiophilus biguttatus is a small (3.5–5.5 mm), black to brassy-coloured beetle with obvious protruding eyes and a parallel-sided body form. The elytra possess two, bright, metallic, brassy-yellow stripes. It is a rapidly-darting, diurnally-active predator.

Life cycle
Adult beetles over-winter and breed in the spring. The next generation of adults is active in the spring and early summer. This beetle is very widely distributed in arable crops and gardens and is possibly associated also with woodland, as are many ground beetles. Some adults have wings, although, as is common in the ground beetles, many do not; this species is however considered to be relatively dispersive. Little is known about larvae which are probably subterranean, and pupation takes place in the soil.

Crop/pest associations
N. biguttatus is a common predator in spring and summer, eating soil invertebrates, especially springtails and aphids on the ground. It is an actively hunting predator and has a pronounced darting gait when disturbed.

Influence on growing practices
N. biguttatus is affected by pesticide sprays in the spring and summer, especially because it is diurnal and active at the time of spray application. If the plant canopy being sprayed is dense and run-off of the spray is avoided, the ground beneath the plant may be protected sufficiently for the insect to survive. Its dispersal power suggests that it might rapidly recolonize sprayed sites, once residues have ameliorated.

POECILUS CUPREUS (LINNAEUS) (139)

Species characteristics
Poecilus cupreus is common in agricultural fields throughout Europe where it prefers relatively moist habitats. The larvae and the adults are polyphagous and consume a variety of prey. Adults of *P. cupreus* are typically bright metallic green in colour but may also be bronze or coppery coloured. The first two antennal segments are a yellow or orange colour. *P. cupreus* is a pterostichine carabid with a wedge-shaped body well adapted to pushing and burrowing its way through soil and leaf litter. Adults are 9–13 mm in length.

Life cycle
P. cupreus is a spring breeding carabid species which over-winters as an adult. Both adults and larvae consume insect prey, although in England the adults will also attack young plants of the genus *Beta*.

Crop/pest associations
P. cupreus is a generalist carabid beetle with no associations known to particular prey types. Common in all field crops this beetle will consume fly eggs and pupae, aphids and soil mites. *P. cupreus* thrives in tall dense vegetation and is often found close to water courses.

Influence on growing practices
Because of its widespread distribution, this species has been used as an indicator for evaluating the effects of pesticides on non-target arthropods. Adults have been found to be susceptible only to the most toxic insecticides and they are generally considered to be robust predators. Hedgerow and uncropped areas around crops provide an over-wintering habitat for many predatory carabid beetle species including *P. cupreus*.

138 *Notiophilus biguttatus* beetle attacking an aphid.

139 *Poecilus cupreus* adult beetle.

PTEROSTICHUS MELANARIUS (ILLIGER) (140, 141)

Species characteristics

Pterostichus melanarius is a large (12–18 mm), stout beetle with a pronotum that is narrower than the elytra and long, sharp mandibles. It is completely black and generally wingless, with two small punctures on the elytra and the bead around the pronotum is widened laterally. A nocturnal species, it shelters under rocks and vegetation in the day and is completely ground-based. *P. melanarius* is very common, found in all kinds of open, damp countryside and in agricultural fields and gardens. A similar predatory carabid, *P. madidus* (Fabricius), can be determined by the rounded hind angle to the pronotum compared to *P. melanarius* which has a sharp hind angle.

Life cycle

Eggs are laid in soil and the larvae are subterranean. Adults and larvae over-winter in fields or grassland and migrate in dry periods by walking from open crop environments to damper, grassier habitats. Some adults may breed in a second year. They can cross more wooded areas, but rarely colonize them. Adults are most common in late summer and are particularly abundant in large agricultural fields where egg laying in open field soil may confer an early competitive advantage to larvae.

Crop/pest associations

P. melanarius is an active, voracious predator eating any carrion or invertebrate prey it can locate, including small earthworms (which may dominate its diet), molluscs, caterpillars and aphids on the ground. It may eat strawberry fruit on occasions, but is not a serious pest.

140 *Pterostichus melanarius* (left) competing with *P. madidus* (right) for a slug.

141 *P. madidus* attacking a slug.

Influence on growing practices

Even if the adults are affected by pesticides, the subterranean larvae are protected from most sprays and other harmful practices. The most damaging chemicals are in slug pellets and overuse of these should be avoided in the garden. Being wingless, rates of population recovery may be slow.

TRECHUS QUADRISTRIATUS (SCHRANK) (142)

Species characteristics

Trechus quadristriatus is a small (3.0–4.0 mm in length), active beetle, brown in colour and distinguished from the similar sized *Bembidion* spp. by the fully developed last segment of the maxillary palps and by the recurrent first elytral stria. It is found on dry, sparsely vegetated terrain and the moist soil of cultivated fields. *T. quadristriatus* is not confined to agricultural habitats and has been found in mountains, sand dunes and in the nests of small mammals. It is often found flying at night in summer.

Life cycle

T. quadristriatus is an autumn breeder with larval hibernation in the soil, although a small number of adults also over-winter.

Crop/pest associations

T. quadristriatus is known primarily as a polyphagous predator capable of feeding on aphids in cereal crops and is present in fields all the year round. *T. quadristriatus* may be particularly important as a predator early in the season when many of the colonist species have not yet arrived and when the first cereal aphids are detected.

Influence on growing practices

Although individual *T. quadristriatus* are sensitive to broad-spectrum insecticides such as dimethoate, *T. quadristriatus* has been shown to survive in crops treated with insecticides in summer as long as the canopy is fully developed. Since larvae over-winter in the soil they are generally protected from winter insecticide use.

142 *Trechus* sp. adult beetle.

Staphylinidae

ORDER: COLEOPTERA
FAMILY: STAPHYLINIDAE
ROVE BEETLES

Adult staphylinid (rove) beetles are easily identified by their short elytra (wing cases) which leave part of their abdomen (usually six segments) exposed (**143–145**). Staphylinids can be active polyphagous predators in agricultural crops but some species are fungal feeders whilst others are parasitoids of fly pupae. The common predatory staphylinids include the larger species such as the devil's coach horse, *Staphylinus olens* (**143**), reaching 32 mm in length and found in the daytime under stones in gardens and woodland. Fungal feeders, detritivores and parasitoid staphylinids are smaller and may be only a few millimetres in length. The smaller species can be extremely difficult to identify and as a consequence they have often been overlooked by entomologists studying their potential as pest control agents.

143 *Staphylinus olens* (Müller) (devil's coach horse) eating a woodlouse.

144 *Tachyporus chrysomelinus* (Linnaeus) feeding on aphids.

145 *Paederus littoralis* (Gravenhorst), a predatory rove beetle with aphid prey.

ALEOCHARINAE (146, 147)

Species characteristics

Aleocharinae are small dark brown or black staphylinid beetles common in detritus and moist organic matter. Adult beetles fly readily and can be distinguished from other staphylinid families because their antennae are inserted on the upper surface of the head near their eyes. There are a great many species of Aleocharinae and field collected specimens are difficult to identify. Some can only be identified by examination of their genitalia. The most frequently collected Aleocharinae in arable crops in northern Europe include *Aloconota gregaria* (Erichson), *Atheta fungi* (Gravenhorst) (agg.) and *Amisha* spp. One species, *Aleochara bilineata*, has been mass-reared for use in biological control of root maggots. *A. bilineata* has also been used as an indicator species for testing the effects of pesticides and has been widely cultured. It is 5–6 mm in length.

Life cycle

Aleocharinae are predatory as adults but many have a parasitoid larval stage. *A. bilineata* lay their eggs in moist soil close to plants infested with root maggots. Larvae hatch after five days and the first instar larvae enter a fly pupa and begin feeding. *Aleochara* spp. pupate within the host pupa and emerge as an adult after 30–40 days. The time for development from egg to adult takes approximately six weeks and there may be two generations per year. *A. bilineata* overwinters as a first instar larva within a host pupa.

Crop/pest associations

Aleocharinae adults and larvae attack the larvae and pupae of root maggots (Diptera: Anthomyiidae), which are found in a wide range of crops, particularly vegetables. The main host species belong to the genera *Delia* and *Hylemya* and include onion fly, wheat bulb fly and cabbage root fly.

Influence on growing practices

Aleocharinae can typically control 30–50% of root fly maggot pupae early in the season and up to 95% late in the season. Broad-spectrum insecticides are harmful to Aleocharinae. Seed dressings give control of the root maggot whilst the parasitoid can enter the root to attack the pupa and avoid toxic residues.

146 *Aleochara bilineata* (Gyllenhal) adult.

147 *A. bilineata* emerging from *Delia radicum* (Linnaeus) (cabbage root fly) pupa.

ATHETA CORIARIA (KRAATZ) (148, 149)

Species characteristics
The adult *Atheta coriaria* is 3–4 mm long and dark brown to black in colour. It flies well, but spends most of the time in the soil or growing medium of the crop. Occasionally it is found on yellow sticky cards, but these seem to be more incidental rather than active catches. Larvae vary from creamy white in the early instars to a yellowish brown in the later instars. All motile life stages are very active and fast moving. They are often seen on the soil surface, but readily enter any crevices, often following the plant stem down below the soil-line.

Life cycle
The entire life cycle of the beetle is spent in the soil where female *A. coriaria* lay their eggs. After hatching they develop through three larval stages, all of which are predatory. The pupal case is composed of soil particles held together by strands of silk. Development time from egg to adult is 21–22 days at 25°C (77°F), decreasing to approximately 11–12 days at 32°C (90°F). There is no recorded diapause. These beetles can be reared on artificial diet, which may also have some potential as a supplement to encourage establishment or movement into desired areas in the glasshouse. At high predator populations, cannibalism has been shown to occur.

Crop/pest associations
A. coriaria are generalist predators that feed and complete development on diets of fungus gnats (eggs, larvae, pupae), shore flies (eggs, larvae, pupae) and thrips (pupae, second stage larvae). When presented with large numbers of prey they will kill more than they eat. Other studies have shown them to feed on a wide range of soil-dwelling insects.

Influence on growing practices
A. coriaria has been shown to establish and thrive in glasshouse crops in a number of different growing media including peat mixes, coconut fiber and rockwool. In commercial glasshouses growing weekly crops, they will readily move into and establish in new plantings. There does not appear to be any effect of irrigation practices (e.g. sub-irrigation versus top irrigation) on beetle populations.

PHILONTHUS COGNATUS (STEPHENS) (150)

Species characteristics
There are 75 species of *Philonthus* in central Europe and they are generally black in colour. The largest of the common species in arable crops, *P. cognatus*, is 9.5–10.5 mm in length and has a pale yellow underside to the first antennal segment. Other *Philonthus* species are smaller but often have two characteristic lines of three setae on the pronotum with a fourth offset seta to each side. Eyes are smaller than the temple and the first antennal segment is longer than the distance between the antennae.

Life cycle
Adult and larvae are predatory, attacking a range of arthropod prey. Adults are often found amongst decaying vegetation from spring to late summer.

Crop/pest associations
Philonthus spp. are amongst the most voracious of the predatory staphylinid beetles commonly found in cultivated fields and agricultural crops. *Philonthus* spp. have been shown to be one of the major aphid predators in cereal crops and together with other polyphagous predators they can limit the size of a cereal aphid outbreak.

Influence on growing practices
Like most of the polyphagous predators *Philonthus* spp. are adversely affected by the use of broad-spectrum insecticides. Provision of over-wintering refugia, such as strips of tussock forming grasses *Holcus anatus* (Linnaeus) and *Dactylis glomerata* (Linnaeus) in and around cereal fields has been shown to increase greatly the abundance of many predatory beetles.

148 *Atheta coriaria* larva.

149 *A. coriaria* adult.

150 *Philonthus cognatus* (rove beetle) adult.

TACHYPORUS SPP. (151, 152)

Species characteristics
Of the *Tachyporus* species found in agricultural crops in northern Europe, *T. hypnorum* (Fabricius) is perhaps the most common and the most easily identified, being 4–5 mm in length with a dark circular marking on the pronotum with a pale surround. Another common species, *T. chrysomelinus* (Linnaeus), has a pale pronotum, as do the less common *T. dispar* and *T. solutus* (Erichson). *Tachyporus* species are identified primarily by their elytral chaetotaxy, requiring high magnification and the appropriate taxonomic keys. Beetles of the genus *Tachyporus* are particularly active in cereal crops at night where they climb the plant in search of aphids and other prey. The characteristic shape of a *Tachyporus* beetle allows it to reach into the space between adjacent cereal grains on the ear and feed on the aphids found there.

Life cycle
Adult *T. hypnorum* can occur in arable crops all the year round but are most numerous in summer. *T. hypnorum* migrates from field margins in mid to late summer, when breeding takes place. The presence of hedgerows as refugia may be particularly important for this species.

Crop/pest associations
Tachyporus is best known as a cereal aphid predator, particularly active against *Sitobion avenae* in the summer months. However, *Tachyporus* species are polyphagous and may also be found in high numbers in orchard crops, gardens, and hedgerows.

Influence on growing practices
Numbers of adults and larvae of *Tachyporus* spp. found in arable crops have declined over the past 20 years. *Tachyporus* spp. are also fungivores, feeding mainly on mildew and rusts, so this decline in numbers may be due to an increase in the use of foliar fungicides. *Tachyporus* spp. are very dispersive and can colonize cropped areas each year. Because they are colonists, particularly to arable crops, *Tachyporus* are not generally exposed to autumn insecticides and herbicides.

XANTHOLINUS SPP. (153)

Species characteristics
Two species of *Xantholinus* (*X. linearis* [Oliver] and *X. longiventris* [Heer]) are commonly found in agricultural crops. In both beetles the body is elongate (6–9 mm) with a narrow neck and with a rounded shape to the back of the head. Both species are dark in colour and have a long first segment to their antennae. Under high magnification the thorax of *X. linearis* has a transverse microsculpture (fingerprint-like pattern) whereas *X. longiventris* is smooth.

Life cycle
Xantholinus spp. adults are found in arable crops from early spring and reach a peak in mid summer before declining. Little is known of the life cycles of individual species of *Xantholinus*.

Crop/pest associations
Xantholinus spp. are polyphagous predators in agricultural crops. The adults are relatively slow moving and feed mostly on Diptera larvae and other less mobile prey. Relatively large numbers of Xantholininae can be found in arable crops and grassland.

Influence on growing practices
Xantholinus spp. are susceptible to broad-spectrum insecticides. They can fly and can recolonize crops relatively quickly. Like many polyphagous predators Xantholininae are not common in very dry habitats. The presence of some ground-covering plants in and around cropped areas will provide refugia with high humidity, which in turn will support predatory species.

Cicindelidae

ORDER: COLEOPTERA
FAMILY: CICINDELIDAE
TIGER BEETLES

CICINDELA CAMPESTRIS (LINNAEUS) (FIELD TIGER BEETLE) (154, 155)

Species characteristics
Tiger beetles are closely related to ground beetles but have their antennae inserted on the top of the head, just in front of the eyes and have no striation on their elytra. The commonest, *Cicindela campestris*, is 10.5–14.5 mm in length, bright metallic green with a pale yellow spot on each elytron and can be seen running on the soil surface on sunny days. An adult *C. campestris* will fly readily when disturbed but usually lands after a short distance.

Life cycle
Adult tiger beetles can be found in fields in warm places from spring to late summer.

Crop/pest associations
Both adults and larvae of *C. campestris* are carnivorous. Larvae make burrows and lie in wait for their prey.

Influence on growing practices
Because of their burrowing habit tiger beetles are generalist predators found only on light, well-drained soils.

151 *Tachyporus chrysomelinus* attacking an aphid.

152 *T. chrysomelinus* (rove beetle) adult.

153 *Xantholinus* sp. (rove beetle) adult.

154 *Cicindela campestris* head and mouth-parts.

155 *C. campestris* adult beetle.

Dermaptera

FORFICULA AURICULARIA (LINNAEUS) (156–158)

Species characteristics

Earwigs are found throughout the world; many species are omnivorous, feeding as predators, scavengers and occasionally as primary plant pests. Adult females are protective to their brood and in some species carry food to the young. The European earwig *Forficula auricularia* is an efficient predator of aphids and insect eggs; they are able to survive with low densities of prey in many situations including cereal, hop and orchard crops. Adults are around 20 mm long with a flattened reddish-brown body. The tip of the abdomen has a pair of pincers which are curved in the male and almost straight in the female. The vein-less forewings (elytra) are short and serve to protect the extremely delicate, folded hindwings. The insect can fly but this is rarely observed. There are several theories concerning the origin of the English name. Some believe that it crawls into ears; it is true that earwigs do search out narrow cracks and passages and come to rest with their dorsal and ventral surfaces in contact with other surfaces. However, they must only rarely occur in ears. A more likely explanation for the name is that it is derived from 'earwing'; the delicate hindwings, when unfolded, resemble the human outer ear (the pinna), and the shape of the wing and pattern of the delicate veins are remarkably like the human ear with its cartilaginous ridges and furrows. The earwig Order, Dermaptera, gives a clue to the second way of describing the forewings, meaning 'skin wing', and the wings strikingly resemble flakes of human epidermis which peel off a few days after severe sunburn! Earwig nymphs resemble adults but have wing buds, not wings, and these are larger at each nymphal moult.

Life cycle

Adults and eggs over-winter and are found below ground in moist, sheltered places. The adults form cells in the soil and the nymphs are protected by the parents. Eggs hatch in early spring and the young nymphs feed on young leaves and other plants; mature adults first appear in early summer. There is one generation each year, although over-wintering females lay eggs which hatch later than those laid in the autumn.

Earwigs are mainly nocturnal, hiding unless disturbed within flowers, leaf sheaths, hollow plant stems, under bark or amongst dense mats of vegetation close to the soil surface. Their climbing ability contributes to their role as predators of pests such as aphids, and has led to the gardening trap of an upturned flower pot on a stick with crumpled paper in the pot; the paper provides the surface contact the insect needs.

Crop/pest associations

Earwigs are mainly scavengers on decaying plant tissue but also take green plant matter and living and dead insects. They are a well recognized pest to many growers, particularly when they damage flowers and leaves; they will also chew fruits borne close to the ground, including strawberries or ripe blackcurrants. In North America they have been the subject of a biological control programme to control numbers. However, they can be important predators of pests such as aphids and, in crops such as hops where aphids are a major problem, the earwig can out-climb other predatory groups. In arable land they also eat aphid pests, but their close association with field boundaries persists through the summer, limiting their bio-control potential compared with more dispersive insects such as the carabid beetles.

156 *Forficula auricularia* adult male.

157 *F. auricularia* adult female.

158 *F. auricularia* adult male.

Influence on growing practices

Earwigs are susceptible to insecticides and to the disruption of their field boundary habitat by cultivation and the removal of perennial grasses; see the ground beetles such as *Demetrias* and *Bembidion* spp.

Diptera

ORDER: DIPTERA
FAMILY: EMPIDIDAE
DANCE FLIES

Insects of the order Diptera have one pair of membranous wings and a pair of minute club-shaped balancing organs called halteres. Adults feed on a liquid diet, either from decaying matter, plant nectar and pollen or, in some species, blood. Most (primitive) larvae have biting mouth-parts or, in advanced species, a pair of specialized hooks that rupture the surface skin from which they can suck the liquid contents. Larvae lack true legs, although some species have fleshy stumps similar to the prolegs of Lepidoptera that aid their wriggling movement.

Many dipterous flies are predatory at some stage in their life cycle, e.g. the larvae of *Aphidoletes aphidimyza* are predatory against many species of aphid while the delicate adult feeds only on honeydew or nectar. Both adult and larva of *Empis tessellata* are predatory but on different hosts for each life stage. Several of the larger Diptera mimic bees and wasps with a striped thorax; however, the lack of a constricted waist and only one pair of wings should indicate from which order it originates.

EMPIS TESSELLATA (FABRICIUS) (159)
EMPIS STERCOREA (160)

Species characteristics
There are over 3,000 known species from this family of flies and having a vast range in size and form can be easily mistaken for other Diptera. Both adult and larvae are predatory on other insects, mainly feeding on other, smaller, adult flies and larvae but they are also frequent visitors to flowers for nectar. Larvae may be found in a wide range of habitats from fresh water ponds to many that live on prey feeding on animal dung, decaying plant matter and in soil. The common name 'dance flies' arises from their courtship displays involving the presentation of prey as a stimulus to mating. At 9–11 mm in length the adults of *Empis tessellata* are among the largest members of the family. The wings are strongly yellowish brown tinted and the adult fly is conspicuous because of its size and dark grey colour. The maggot-like larvae are creamy-yellow and feed with internal mouth hooks; they reach 13–14 mm when fully grown.

Life cycle
E. tessellata occurs throughout Europe while other members of the genus *Empis* are found throughout the world. The adult flies occur through the summer months and are common and widely distributed in fields, pastures, wetlands and lightly wooded areas. The larvae live in the soil and leaf litter and like the adults are also predatory, feeding on other soft-bodied arthropods. The diet of the larvae consists most probably of other fly larvae that occur commonly in soils. Little is known of the biology of *E. tessellata* and the overwintering stage is unknown.

Crop/pest associations
Many empid flies including *E. tessellata* have been reported as important predators of agricultural pests, principally of flies such as leaf miners and other midges but also of other plant-feeding insects such as aphids and plant bugs. However, many empids are highly predatory but their precise role has not been fully documented.

Influences on growing practices
Little is known of the biology of *E. tessellata* or other empids, but frequently cultivated soils will upset their breeding sites. The adult flies are susceptible to pesticide sprays.

159 *Empis tessellata* (dance fly) and aphids.

160 *Empis stercorea* (dance fly).

Cecidomyiidae

ORDER: DIPTERA
FAMILY: CECIDOMYIIDAE
PREDATORY MIDGES

The majority of insects in this family are gall forming midges capable of considerable plant damage. However, some are notable predators particularly of aphids and spider mites. Many species are found throughout the world and have been extensively studied for their commercial value as both mass-produced and naturally occurring predators. The larvae are the only predacious stage and can kill far more prey than they consume which makes them an extremely useful bio-insecticide. Recent research has shown that adult midges produce more viable eggs when they feed on pest honeydew or plant nectar than when water alone is available.

APHIDOLETES APHIDIMYZA (RONDANI) (161–164)

Species characteristics
Adult *Aphidoletes aphidimyza* closely resemble miniature mosquitoes, having long legs and delicate wings; females have bead-like antennae, while in males antennae are feathery and cover the length of the body. Adults are nocturnal but can be found hanging in shady places on plants and pots during the day. Larvae are the most noticeable stage with their orange colouration; under magnification white fat bodies can be clearly seen. *A. aphidimyza* feeding on black aphids have a darker orange appearance.

Life cycle
Oval, shiny orange/red eggs (0.3 × 0.1 mm) are deposited close to aphid colonies. On hatching the larvae are of similar size and for the first few days are difficult to find. The young larvae feed on honeydew and also directly on the host aphids. Before feeding on an aphid, it is paralysed by an injection of toxin, usually in the leg. The larva then begins sucking out the body juices from underneath the aphid. The larva then begins sucking out the juices from underneath the aphid. After 7–10 days the larvae are about 2.5 mm in length and clearly visible amongst the aphids. When fully grown the larvae drop from the leaf and form a cocoon of grains of sand and pupate within. Emergence is usually about 10–14 days later providing the pupating medium does not desiccate.

Crop/pest associations
A. aphidimyza is predatory on all the common glasshouse aphids and many outdoor species; prey consumption ranges from 5–10 up to 80–100 per larva. Aphids die after an attack and when in large numbers many aphids are killed by injection of toxin but are not eaten. Dead aphids remain attached to the leaf but frequently fall off when they begin to decay, leaving a relatively clean plant.

Influence on growing practices
The adults are nocturnal and require a period of darkness for mating and oviposition. Consequently in areas of continuous lighting such as airports, shopping malls and some office atriums this predator does not work well. Conversely, the larvae require at least 15.5 h of light to prevent the pupae from entering diapause, although very low intensity light has been shown to be sufficient for this purpose. Adults are more susceptible to pesticides than larvae and the selective aphicide pirimicarb is also harmful to the adult. Banker plants of cereal, such as barley, rye and wheat are often infested with a specific cereal aphid (*Rhopalosiphum padi* or *Sitobian avenae*) to produce many beneficials *in situ*.

161 Head-on view of an *Aphidoletes aphidimyza* midge.

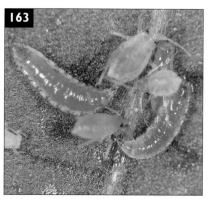

162 *A. aphidimyza* larvae preying on *Macrosiphoniella sanborni* (chrysanthemum aphids).

163 *A. aphidimyza* larvae preying on *Myzus persicae* (peach–potato aphids).

164 *A. aphidimyza* adult midge.

FELTIELLA ACARISUGA (VALLOT) (165–171)

Species characteristics
Visually similar to the aphid predatory midge *Aphidoletes aphidimyza* in both adult and larval stages, only the larvae of this cecidomyiid midge are predatory. Unlike *A. aphidimyza*, *Feltiella acarisuga* pupates on the leaf in a white silken web. It is this habit which has caused restrictions in the mass production for commercial use of this insect.

Life cycle
Orange/red eggs are laid amongst spider mite colonies which, after 3–5 days, hatch to minute orange coloured larvae. These feed on all stages of spider mite and can eat up to 15 eggs, 5 young or 3 mature mites each day. After a further 5–7 days (at 22°C [72°F]) the fully developed larva spins a silken cocoon, usually against the side of a leaf vein, in which a pupa is formed. White silken cocoons are generally found on the underside of leaves; an almost transparent skin protruding from one end indicates that the adult has emerged.

Crop/pest associations
Little is known about the fecundity or host-searching ability of this predator other than it appears in large numbers some years and rarely in others. In most instances it is found where biological control is being used for other pests and pesticide usage is restricted. *F. acarisuga* can be parasitized by an *Aphanogmus* species of wasp, which attacks the larval stage and emerges as an adult from the cocoon. This makes it difficult to distinguish between healthy predator cocoons and those carrying a parasitoid.

Influence on growing practices
F. acarisuga prefers humidity of about 85% but is more effective and tolerant to low humidities than *Phytoseiulus persimilis*. The presence of aphid or whitefly honeydew as a food source for adults has shown increased fecundity. As the predator pupates within a cocoon attached to a leaf, heavy de-leafing of glasshouse tomato crops may deplete their numbers. Combined introductions with polyphagous predators such as *Chrysoperla* and *Macrolophus* spp. are not recommended as the slow moving larvae frequently fall victim as prey.

165 *Feltiella acarisuga* larva feeding on a spider mite.

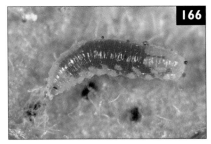

166 *F. acarisuga* coloured red having fed on diapausal *Tetranychus urticae* (2-spotted spider mites).

167 *F. acarisuga* cocoon.

168 Adult *F. acarisuga* emerging from a cocoon.

169 *F. acarisuga* midge.

170 *F. acarisuga* cocoon parasitized by a hyperparasitoid wasp *Aphanogmus* sp.

171 *F. acarisuga* cocoon opened to show the pupa of a hyperparasitoid wasp *Aphanogmus* sp.

Syrphidae

Hoverflies (**172–177**) are closely associated with woodland habitats but have adapted to man-made environments and are commonly found in gardens and agricultural crops where flowering plants and aphids occur. Adult hoverflies feed primarily on nectar and pollen but will also consume aphid honeydew. Larvae of many hoverflies are voracious predators of aphids. Commoner hoverfly species attack a wide range of aphid species, whereas the rarer hoverflies are more restricted in their prey species. Only hoverflies of the subfamily Syrphinae are aphid predators. Other hoverflies have very diverse larval feeding habits. Adults of the commoner hoverflies are easily identified by the patterns of their body markings.

Most hoverflies are mimics of bees and wasps, and share the aposematic (warning) colouration of many of these Hymenoptera. They are, however, true flies (order: Diptera) and are therefore the only insect order to have one pair of wings. This fly family has a characteristic 'false vein' (*vena spuria*) in the wing that can be seen with a hand lens or a binocular microscope.

172 An adult *Episyrphus balteatus* on a composite flower.

173 Hoverfly egg laid among a colony of aphids.

174 Several hoverfly larvae on a rose (photograph courtesy of Rosie Mayer/Holt Studios).

175 Hoverfly larva among *Dysaphis plantaginea* (Passerini) (rosy-apple aphid).

176 Hoverfly larva feeding on an aphid (photograph courtesy of Duncan Smith/Holt Studios).

177 Adult *Sphaerophoria scripta* (Linnaeus) male fly on an umbellifer flower.

EPISYRPHUS BALTEATUS (DEGEER) (178–182)

Species characteristics
The abdomen of *Episyrphus balteatus* is banded black and dull orange. The eyes of the male touch on the dorsal surface of the head; those of the female are separated. The adults hover over flowers and aphid colonies.

Life cycle
Both adults and the pupal stage over-winter. Both sexes take pollen and nectar from wild and garden plants from early spring onwards (an important aspect for their enhancement in crops); the females need the amino acids from pollen to mature their eggs, while both sexes use the nectar for energy. Eggs are laid in, or close to, aphid colonies. Maggot-like larvae hatch in a few and voraciously consume aphids, several hundred of these being eaten during larval development. Larvae are mainly nocturnal feeders so are not so easily seen during the daytime, as they shelter behind leaf sheaths. Pear-shaped pupae are fixed to the plant and the adults emerge after a few days. Spring adults may give rise to two more generations before autumn.

Most gardeners see hoverfly adults on or near flowers with an open structure; these short-tongued insects can easily obtain nectar and pollen from such plants, especially in the families Compositae, Umbelliferae, Cheopodievea and (pollen only) Aramineae (grasses). They can be very abundant in late summer, as are 7-spot ladybirds, as adults of both predators emigrate from ripening cereals which had earlier supported high aphid and predator populations.

Crop/pest associations
Some hoverflies feed as larvae on decaying organic matter or occur in stagnant water, but the species useful in bio-control (including *E. balteatus*) are aphid-feeders as larvae. *E balteatus* larvae are common in arable crops, as well as in horticulture and gardens and feed on a wide range of aphid species. They are less common on shrubs and trees, although hoverflies do occupy this niche.

Influence on growing practices
E. balteatus will lay eggs at very low aphid densities, but of course 'insurance' pesticide sprays will kill them. Pyrethroid insecticides are relatively less harmful to them than are some organophosphate and carbamate products. The dependence of the adults on floral resources means that mis-managed field boundaries, in which annual weeds take the place of other dicotyledonous plants which provide pollen, offer few resources in spring. Drilling field margins with strips of pollen-rich plants, such as tansey-leaf (*Phacelia tanacetifolia*), buckwheat (*Fagopyrum esculentum*) or Umbelliferae such as coriander (*Coriandrum sativum* [Linnaeus]) can enhance populations of adult hoverflies in adjacent fields, resulting in a higher rate of egg laying and of aphid predation.

181 *E. balteatus* pupa.

182 *E. balteatus* adult.

178 *Episyrphus balteatus* laying her eggs among a colony of *Macrosiphum rosae* (rose aphids) on a rose.

179 *E. balteatus* eggs among a *M. rosae* colony on a rose.

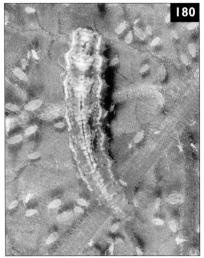

180 *E. balteatus* larva with aphids.

183 *Scaeva pyrastri* adult.

184 *S. pyrastri* adult.

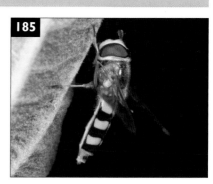

185 *Syrphus ribesii* adult.

SCAEVA PYRASTRI (LINNAEUS) (183, 184)

Species characteristics

Adult *Scaeva* species are large and distinctive with three pairs of white markings on a black abdomen, the middle pair crescent shaped. *Scaeva* spp. larvae are aphid predators and feed on a wide range of prey species. Eggs are oblong, white in colour and about 1 mm in length.

Life cycle

Scaeva pyrastri is polyvoltine, with three to four generations per year and with the adult females over-wintering. In mild seasons it is not uncommon to see these flies active throughout the winter months. Eggs are laid from early spring onwards amongst aphid colonies. Larvae develop as they feed on the aphid colony and pupate on the ground beneath the crop. Emerging adults often migrate and can cover large distances in search of suitable aphid-rich sites for egg laying.

Crop/pest associations

Because it over-winters as an adult, *Scaeva* spp. can appear early in the season and lay eggs amongst the first aphid colonies to appear in crops. Although larvae attack many aphid species, *Scaeva* spp. are considered to be important predators of *Rhopalosiphum insertum* in fruit orchards early in the season, and of *Dysaphis plantaganea* from spring to mid summer.

Influence on growing practices

As for all hoverflies the provision of sources of pollen and nectar helps adults to feed and to mature their ovaries and produce eggs. Broad-spectrum insecticides used against aphids are toxic to adults and larvae of *S. pyrastri* and other hoverfly species. Selective aphicides, such as pirimicarb, are less harmful to larvae and adults of hoverflies.

SYRPHUS RIBESII (LINNAEUS) (185–187)

Species characteristics

Syrphus ribesii is a widespread and common hoverfly species, with characteristic yellow abdominal markings. Larvae can be identified by the shape of their breathing tubes and by their colouration, but are best recognized by the adult stage. Adult males stationary on twigs or foliage can produce a high pitched sound, using their flight muscles to raise their body temperature.

Life cycle

Females lay eggs in or near aphid colonies during the summer. Larvae are voracious predators of aphids in many agricultural crops and in gardens, piercing the aphid's body and sucking the contents dry. While feeding the larvae often raise their mouthparts and lift the aphid off the plant. The larval stage of *S. ribesii* can be as short as ten days and under favourable conditions there can be as many as three generations per year. *S. ribesii* over-winters mostly as a larva on the ground or hidden in vegetation. In spring the larva pupates and after a few days the adult emerges. However, in autumn many *Syrphus* species adults avoid winter by migrating south to the Mediterranean.

Crop/pest associations

S. ribesii is an important aphid predator in orchard and broad acre agricultural crops and also occurs in gardens. An individual larva can eat more than a thousand aphids during its development. Adult *S. ribesii* adults have particularly short mouth-parts so they can only feed on pollen of very open flowers.

Influence on growing practices

Provision of flowering plants as pollen and nectar sources has been shown to encourage hoverflies. Compositae and Umbelliferae are thought to be the most useful plant families for this purpose. Two species with a high availability of pollen and nectar for the flies and a readily available supply of seeds are *Phacelia tanacetifolia* (Benth.) (Hydrophyllaceae) and *Fagopyrum esculentum* (Moench) (Polygonaceae). Hoverfly larvae are sensitive to most broad-spectrum insecticides but are not generally affected by fungicides.

186 Female *S. ribesii* hoverfly on a flower.

187 Male *S. ribesii* hoverfly on *Phacelia* sp. flower.

Heteroptera

ORDER: HEMIPTERA
SUBORDER: HETEROPTERA
PREDATORY BUGS

Heteroptera are so named for their wings, having 'different' forms: a hard leathery basal area and membranous tip. These insects are all noticeable for having piercing mouth-parts with many being plant pests often causing severe damage. However, several are very active predators feeding on a wide range of organisms. Eggs are laid into plant tissues, often leaving a small raised blister-like opercula visible on the surface; after depositing eggs adults frequently feed from the plant wound. There are many predatory species from several families that are generalists, attacking a wide range of prey species often as plant or habitat specialists (**188–191**). Feeding begins when the grooved rostrum or proboscis selects a suitable site for the mandibular stylets within to penetrate, rasp and cut the prey tissue before the maxillary stylets enter the wound. These delicate needle-like tubes are protected within the mandibular stylets and form canals that deliver saliva containing proteolytic enzymes and remove pre-digested liquefied prey contents. However, in the absence of insect or mite prey they are able to survive on plant sap and pollen; many are able to penetrate human skin to give a small 'bite'.

188 *Orius niger* adult feeding on a *Myzus persicae* (Salzer) (peach–potato aphid).

189 *Deraeocoris* sp. feeding on *Aphis pomi*.

190 *Deraeocoris* sp. feeding on *Eriosoma lanigerum* (Hausmann) (wooly aphids).

191 *Deraeocoris* sp. feeding on *A. pomi* (De Geer) (apple aphids).

ANTHOCORIS NEMORALIS (FABRICIUS) (192)

Species characteristics
Nymph and adult *Anthocoris nemoralis* are entirely carnivorous and are active predators of aphids, spider mites and psyllids. Common throughout Europe on wild and cultivated shrubs, bushes and trees, *A. nemoralis* may become very abundant on commercially managed or neglected fruit trees. Neglected orchards typically contain very high numbers of *A. nemoralis* for one or two years after being abandoned, after which time they become scarce. Adult *A. nemoralis* are distinguished from *A. nemorum* by the colouration of the second and third antennal segments. Antennae are shorter than those of *A. nemorum*.

Life cycle
There are two generations per year. Adults over-winter beneath bark, among dead leaves and in hedgerows. Females emerge from hibernation and lay eggs from spring to early summer. Eggs are inserted into the leaf near to the mid vein, often in groups. Freshly laid eggs are white, turning reddish brown shortly before the emergence of the nymph. The first instar nymph is clear or yellow in colour. Subsequent instars are reddish brown in colour.

Crop/pest associations
A. nemoralis is known as a predator of fruit tree red spider mite in apple orchards, but also attacks aphids and psyllids in many crops. It tends to prefer small prey items.

Influence on growing practices
Increased plant diversity, particularly with flowering plants, in and adjacent to orchards can provide alternative food sources and refugia as well as suitable over-wintering sites. Anthocorid bugs (*Anthocoris* and *Orius* spp.) are usually less sensitive to pesticides than mirid bugs.

193 *Anthocoris nemorum* adult feeding on *Myzus cerasi* (Fabricius) (black cherry aphid).

ANTHOCORIS NEMORUM (LINNAEUS) (193)

Species characteristics
Anthocoris nemorum is similar to *A. nemoralis* in appearance and in habits, but the antennae are longer than those of *A. nemoralis*. Dark parts of the forewings are matt in appearance.

Life cycle
There are two or three generations per year. Adults over-winter beneath bark, among dead leaves and in hedgerows. Females emerge from hibernation and lay eggs from spring to early summer. Females lay about two eggs per day. Eggs are inserted into the leaf near to the mid vein, often in groups up to eight. There are five nymphal stages and the first instar is clear or pale yellow. Subsequent instars are reddish brown in colour.

Crop/pest associations
A. nemorum is a common, naturally occurring predator on trees and shrubs. In fruit orchards *A. nemorum* attacks a wide range of insect and mite prey and has been observed feeding on the sessile larvae of the predatory ladybird *Stethorus punctillum*. *A. nemorum* feeds by piercing its prey from the side with its short rostrum and then sucking out the body contents. Adults consume on average 50 spider mites per day.

Influence on growing practices
The presence of flowering plants under trees and in orchard margins can provide alternative prey and lead to increased numbers of these predators. *A. nemorum* is commonly found on blackberries in the autumn. Brambles and hedgerow plants can provide important over-wintering sites for *A. nemorum*.

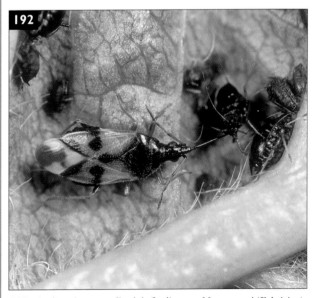

192 *Anthocoris nemoralis* adult feeding on *Myzus cerasi* (Fabricius) (black cherry aphid).

ATRACTOTOMUS MALI (MEYER-DUER) (194, 195)

Species characteristics
Atractotomus mali is a small predatory insect found on hawthorn and apple trees, more frequently in neglected orchards. Adults have a characteristic appearance and are black or reddish brown with a covering of fine white hairs. Males are 3.0–3.5 mm long, females are 3.3–4.0 mm long. In nymphs and adults the second antennal segment is enlarged and is dark while the third and fourth antennal segments are pale and slender.

Life cycle
One generation occurs per year. Eggs are laid in bark, often in clusters and over-winter, hatching in the spring. Nymphs are active from early to mid summer and adults begin to appear from mid summer onwards.

Crop/pest associations
A. mali attacks spider mites, other mites and occasionally aphids and moth larvae in fruit crops throughout Europe. *A. mali* can also be partly phytophagous.

Influence on growing practices
A. mali prefers neglected or low-input orchards and is generally more abundant where there are established hedgerows close to an orchard.

194 *Atractotomus mali* adult.

195 *A. mali* adult.

196 *Blepharidopterus angulatus* adult (photograph courtesy of David V. Alford).

BLEPHARIDOPTERUS ANGULATUS (FALLÉN) (196)

Species characteristics
Blepharidopterus angulatus is commonly known as the black-kneed capsid because of dark spots at the base of each tibia. Formerly one of the commonest predators in apple orchards in southern England, *B. angulatus* has become scarce in recent years. *B. angulatus* is a localized predator of spider mites and small insects in fruit trees, particularly apple, pear, plum and cherry. It is also found on many other tree species. The dark spot is present in nymphs and adults. Males are 5.1–5.7 mm in length, females are 5.7–5.8 mm long.

Life cycle
There is one generation per year. Eggs are laid deep into one- or two-year-old wood and are usually laid singly. A characteristic bump in the wood develops around the egg about three days after laying. *B. angulatus* over-winters in the egg stage. Nymphs begin to emerge from early to mid summer and are yellow to green in colour with red eyes. There are five instars. Adults are bright green with brown antennae, males are larger and darker than females.

Crop/pest associations
B. angulatus is a voracious predator of *Panonychus ulmi* (fruit tree red spider mite) preferring to attack adult female mites. It takes about three minutes for an adult to suck dry an adult female spider mite. A single *B. angulatus* can consume as many as 4300 mites during its lifetime with as many as 3000 of these being consumed by the adult. Although primarily carnivorous, like many mirid bugs *B. angulatus* can feed on plant material, particularly rotten fruits on trees or on the ground.

Influence on growing practices
B. angulatus commonly lays eggs in the wood of *Alnus glutinosa* and *Betula alba*. Suitable tree species in margins of orchards may encourage oviposition. *B. angulatus* is highly sensitive to pesticides.

DERAEOCORIS RUBER (LINNAEUS) (197–199)

Species characteristics
Adult *Deraeocoris ruber* are large (7.0 mm in length), light brown or black in colour with red flashes on the cuneus. Nymphs are crimson reddish with a characteristically wide abdomen bearing black spines.

Life cycle
D. ruber has one generation a year. Eggs are laid singly in one- or two-year-old wood in late summer and hatch from early to mid summer. Adults appear throughout the summer months and into early autumn.

Crop/pest associations
Adults and nymphs are active predators of aphids, particularly the woolly apple aphid *Eriosoma lanigerum*, but also feed on psyllids and mites in apple and pear orchards. Nymphs can occur in large numbers but adults disperse and are rarely found at levels greater than five individuals per tree. *D. ruber* is entirely predatory and can attack other predators and is cannibalistic.

Influence on growing practices
D. ruber is more frequently found in weedy orchards, particularly if there are nettles present under the trees or in the margins. It is rarely found in orchards with bare earth strips beneath trees.

199 *D. ruber* adult about to fly (photograph courtesy of Peter Wilson/Holt Studios).

HETEROTOMA PLANICORNIS (PALLAS) (200–202)

Species characteristics
Heterotoma planicornis is commonly found in neglected orchards throughout Europe. Males are 4.6–5.3 mm in length, females are 4.9–5.5 mm. Adults are purple to dark red in colour with a long thin body and characteristic enlarged and flattened second antennal segments. Nymphs are red in colour and also have an enlarged second antennal segment.

Life cycle
H. planicornis have one generation a year. Eggs are laid in late summer into young wood. Eggs hatch from late spring to mid summer. Adults appear throughout the summer months and into early autumn.

Crop/pest associations
Adults and nymphs are active predators of spider mites and aphids in apple and pear orchards. High numbers have been observed together with outbreaks of pear Psylla. *H. planicornis* is partly phytophagous and leaves and fruits may be attacked.

Influence on growing practices
H. planicornis is more frequently found in orchards with an under-storey of mixed vegetation. Like *Deraeocoris ruber* it appears to favour orchards where nettles are present, either under the trees or in the margins.

197 *Deraeocoris ruber* nymph.

198 *D. ruber* nymph.

200 *Heterotoma planicornis* nymph.

201 *H. planicornis* nymph.

202 *H. planicornis* adult.

MACROLOPHUS CALIGINOSUS (WAGNER) (203–205)

Species characteristics
Macrolophus caliginosus is a polyphagous predatory mirid occurring naturally in a wide range of crops throughout the Mediterranean region. Adults are green, 6.0 mm in length with long legs and antennae that have a black first segment. Nymphs are green to yellowish-green and are found mainly on the underside of leaves. All mobile stages are predatory against a range of small invertebrates including glasshouse whitefly (*Trialeurodes vaporariorum*), tobacco whitefly (*Bemisia tabaci*), aphids, thrips, moth eggs and spider mites.

Life cycle
M. caliginosus is mainly found on plants of the Compositae and Solanaceae families in which adult females lay their eggs. The eggs are inserted deeply in the plant stems and leaves with just a tiny flag visible by hand lens. Development is relatively slow (30 days at 25°C [77°F] increasing to 50 days at 20°C [68°F]) compared to their principal prey, whitefly (22 days at 25°C [77°F] and 30 days at 20°C [68°F]). However, *M. caliginosus* are partly phytophagous which helps their early inoculative release on protected crops before pest levels begin to establish.

Crop/pest associations
M. caliginosus is commercially available as a glasshouse predator of whitefly and other pests. Research has shown that greater than four times more eggs are produced when the predator has whitefly in their diet than when feeding on plant sap alone. Under ideal conditions of suitable host plant, plentiful food supply and reasonably high temperatures the predator can become a plant pest, particularly on cherry tomatoes where fruit loss has been observed. They are not

recommended on gerbera due to flower damage, or cucumber and pepper due to poor establishment.

Influence on growing practices
Additional pest control agents such as *Encarsia formosa* for whitefly are required during the early part of the season while *M. caliginosus* establishes. Diapause under short day lengths does not seem to be a problem as females collected during mid winter in the south of France had ripe eggs in their ovaries. Like all Miridae the adults and nymphs are sensitive to most insecticides, whilst the eggs are protected within the leaf or stem. Short persistence chemicals can therefore be used to reduce predator numbers when crop damage is suspected without eliminating the bug altogether.

203 *Macrolophus caliginosus* nymph with *Trialeurodes vaporariorum* (glasshouse whitefly) scales and pupae.

204 *M.caliginosus* nymph.

205 *M. caliginosus* adult.

ORIUS LAEVIGATUS (LINNAEUS) (206–208)

Species characteristics
Orius laevigatus is a common and important predator of aphids, thrips and spider mites in orchards and in glasshouse vegetable production. It is similar to *O. majusculus* but smaller (2.2–2.5 mm in length), and is similar to several other *Orius* species (*O. minutus*, *O. vicinus*, *O. horvathi*), and it is necessary to examine the genitalia to identify these species occurring in the wild. *Orius* spp. are commonly called flower bugs as they are usually found close to, or within, flowers where they feed on insects, mites and pollen.

Life cycle
Two generations occur per year in northern Europe and three per year in Mediterranean regions. Eggs are laid in groups of three to four in the mid vein on the underside of leaves. Eggs hatch from spring onwards with nymphs and adults being found continuously until autumn.

Crop/pest associations
Adults and nymphs are voracious predators and are commercially available as biological control agents all year round. When prey is scarce *O. laevigatus* has been known to feed on predatory mites.

208 *O. laevigatus* adult feeding on *F. occidentalis.*

Influence on growing practices
O. laevigatus is commercially available as a biological control agent and is sold primarily for introduction into glasshouses. *O. laevigatus* can feed on Lepidoptera eggs when alternative food is scarce.

206 *Orius laevigatus* nymph feeding on *Frankliniella occidentalis* (western flower thrips).

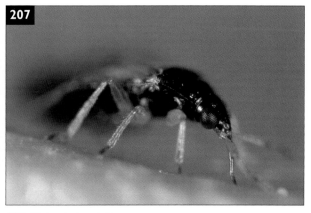

207 *O. laevigatus* adult.

ORIUS MAJUSCULUS (REUTER) (209–212)

Species characteristics
Orius majusculus is a common and important predator of aphids, thrips and spider mites in neglected and commercial orchards. Adults are small (2.6–3.8 mm in length) and with flattened, rounded bodies, very similar in appearance to *O. minutus.*

Life cycle
Females emerge from hibernation through the spring months. Eggs are laid in groups of three to four in the mid vein on the underside of leaves. Eggs hatch from spring onwards with nymphs and adults being found continuously until autumn. The time from oviposition to adult emergence varies from 24–40 days. There are typically two or three generations per year.

Crop/pest associations
Adults and nymphs are active predators of mites and small insects. If fruit tree red spider mites are present in high numbers they will be the preferred prey with all stages being attacked. If prey is scarce they are cannibalistic. Adult *O. majusculus* consume about 35 adult mites per day and nymphs consume about 22 adult mites per day.

Influence on growing practices
Adults and nymphs of all Heteroptera are susceptible to broad-spectrum insecticides. Eggs are generally protected in the leaf mid vein. Where insecticides are used then those which are active for a short period are less damaging than persistent products. The use of microbial insecticides such as *Bacillus thuringiensis* reduces the risk to many predators. The presence of patches of wild flowering plants, either under the trees or in a part of the orchard, can provides a refuge for recolonization when toxic sprays are used, and can provide an alternative source of food when prey is scarce on the trees.

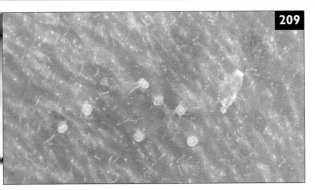

209 *Orius* sp. eggs.

210 *Orius majusculus* nymph feeding on *Frankliniella occidentalis* (western flower thrips).

211 *O. majusculus* nymph feeding on *F. occidentalis*.

212 *O. majusculus* adult feeding on *F. occidentalis*.

PILOPHORUS PERPLEXUS (DOUGLAS AND SCOTT) (213, 214)

Species characteristics
At first sight these predatory bugs resemble ants, both in their colouration and in their movements. The adult *Pilophorus perplexus* is 4.0–4.9 mm in length, dark brown in colour with two conspicuous white bands across the forewings. Nymphs are also dark brown with a broad white spot at the base of the abdomen. Both adults and the nymphs run up and down branches rapidly in search of prey. *P. perplexus* has been observed as an abundant predator on fruit trees where ants were also active.

Life cycle
P. perplexus has one generation a year. Eggs are laid in late summer and over-winter, hatching in spring to early summer. Adults appear from mid to late summer.

Crop/pest associations
Adults and nymphs are active predators of aphids, particularly *Aphis pomi* in apples, but also feed voraciously on Lepidoptera larvae, psyllids and mites in fruit orchards. *P. perplexus* is also commonly found on oak and other deciduous trees.

Influence on growing practices
P. perplexus is usually more common in orchards with established hedgerow margins and may also favour uncropped refugia of wild plants.

213 *Pilophorus perplexus* nymph.

214 *P. perplexus* adult.

PODISUS MACULIVENTRIS (SAY) (215–218)

Species characteristics

Podisus maculiventris is a predatory shield bug found from Canada to Mexico and may be known specifically as the spined soldier bug or generally as stinkbugs (as an odour is released when attacked or squeezed). Adults are 9–13 mm long with prominent spines on the broad 'shoulders' situated just behind the head. Several similar looking shield bugs are pests of plants and may be differentiated from *P. maculiventris* by the presence of a distinctive dark patch on the tip of each forewing. Adults and larvae possess a long pointed proboscis to stab and carry their prey; it is kept folded under the body when not in use for feeding.

Life cycle

Adult females can produce several hundred eggs in groups of 10–30 at a time. These can be deposited on leaves or stems of plants, usually in close proximity to their prey. The eggs hatch after a few days to bright red and black nymphs that become more colourful as they mature. First instar nymphs remain together in a cluster after emerging and are reported not to feed on insect prey. Older nymphs are voracious feeders and can be cannibalistic when prey is scarce.

Crop/pest associations

Young nymphs may be found feeding together from the same prey, particularly if it is a large caterpillar. Larger *P. maculiventris* can be seen running around with a prey body harpooned on their proboscis and may feed from the same larva until most of the juices are consumed. Good control of Colorado potato beetle (*Leptinotarsa decemlineata*) has been achieved in several countries and, more recently, with control of caterpillars on protected crops in Europe.

Influence on growing practices

This predator prefers a warm environment with temperatures above 18°C (64°F) for continual development. They require a source of plant sap in their diet and are not reported as causing any significant plant damage during feeding. Their main host plant range includes cucurbits, aubergine, pepper, potato and tomato. Being polyphagous predators they will feed on other beneficial organisms as well as pest species.

216 *P. maculiventris* nymph feeding on a *Lacanobia oleracea* (tomato moth) caterpillar.

217 *P. maculiventris* adult stylet inserted in a *L. oleracea* caterpillar.

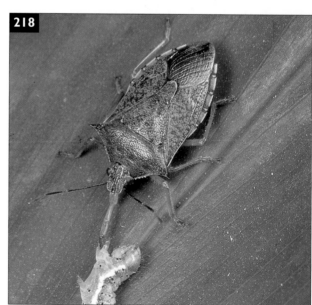

218 *P. maculiventris* adult feeding on a *L. oleracea* caterpillar.

215 *Podisus maculiventris* nymph feeding on a dipteran larva.

Hymenoptera

ORDER: HYMENOPTERA
PARASITOID WASPS

This extremely large order contains many commonly known insects, such as ants, bees and wasps (**219–224**). They usually have two pairs of membranous wings: the rear pair are smaller than the front pair, and have a row of minute hooks along their front edge that attach the two together. Due to reduced venation and large cells the wings may appear transparent. There are two suborders: the Symphyta (whose adults have no waist but larvae have well developed heads and thoracic legs [sawflies]) and the Apocrita (which has a constricted waist between the thorax and abdomen giving the characteristic wasp appearance). The waist is formed by a ring-like second abdominal segment (petiole) that gives considerable abdominal flexibility (see *Aphidius* ovipositing [**219**, **223**]) enabling adult wasps to oviposit in a confined space. The larvae are legless and have a reduced head with relatively simple mouthparts. This is due to the close proximity of their food source: as gall-forming plant feeders that are surrounded by their food, as an ectoparasitoid (*Diglyphus isaea*) where the larva develops directly next to its host or, most commonly, as an endoparasitoid within the host body (*Aphidius* spp.). Mature larvae spin a silken cocoon within the host body to form a 'mummy' (so named after Egyptian mummies that contain a body wrapped in bandages), in which it pupates (**220–222**). Most mummies are golden brown in colour although a few are black (**224**, **227**, **228**), which may speed up development by better utilization of solar heat.

There are two divisions within the Apocrita: the Aculeata, to which ants, bees and wasps belong, are characterized by having their ovipositor modified as a sting; and the Parasitica, which are nearly all parasitoids, with ovipositors adapted for piercing host tissues.

Many parasitoids extend their longevity and fecundity by feeding on host hemolymph after causing a wound with their mandibles or, more commonly, with their ovipositor. Host feeding can result in as many individual hosts killed by adult feeding as by parasitism. This can viewed as a form of predation. When the ovipositor is used to inflict a wound, the adult parasitoid may feed directly as hemolymph oozes out. Others puncture the host and allow the fluid hemolymph to coagulate around the ovipositor, forming a straw-like tube from which she feeds. Host feeding is usually necessary for continued egg production and sustaining oviposition. Adult parasitoids that have been starved (host scarcity or in the case of commercial supplies, those that have been delayed in transit for several days) can resorb their eggs to maintain longevity and must host feed to resume oviposition.

Multiple parasitism occurs when females of more than one species oviposit in the same host individual, as may occur among aphid colonies being attacked by different parasitoids. Similarly, super-parasitism occurs when more eggs of the same species are deposited to an individual host than can reach maturity, regardless of whether laid by a single or several females. Polyembryony, on the other hand, is the development of multiple individuals from a single egg that in some species can produce over 1,000 larvae. Hyperparasitism occurs when one parasitoid species develops as a parasitoid of another parasitoid – an example is shown with an *Aphidius colemani* mummy. Compare the smooth cut exit hole at the rear of the host from the primary parasitoid to the jagged edge exit hole at the top of the host produced by the hyperparasitoid.

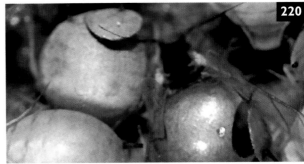

220 Exit holes of *Aphidius* spp. wasps from aphid 'mummies'.

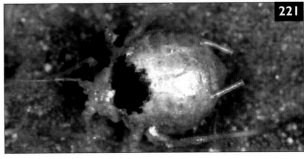

219 *Aphidius ervi* wasp among *Aulacorthum circumflexum* (mottled arum aphids).

221 Aphid mummy showing the jagged exit hole after hyperparasitoid emergence.

222 *Metapolophium dirhodum* (rose–grain aphid) mummy parasitized by an *Aphidius* sp. wasp.

223 An aphid's view of a parasitic wasp *Aphidius* sp. about to lay her eggs.

224 *Encarsia formosa* recently hatched from a parasitized glasshouse whitefly pupa.

ANAGRUS ATOMUS (LINNAEUS) (225, 226)

Species characteristics
Anagrus atomus is a minute orange/red wasp (0.6 mm long) with feathery wings (which are also 0.6 mm long when fully extended) and antennae. The adults are very delicate and short lived, emerging from the pupal stage with a full complement of eggs which they deposit as quickly as possible. Adults are capable of flight but tend to run rapidly over the leaf surface making short flights or jumps from leaf to leaf.

Life cycle
Leafhoppers insert their eggs into secondary veins on the underside of leaves and the parasitoid lays its egg into the eggs of the leafhopper. Initially nothing is visible as the host egg is transparent, but after a few days the minute red eyes of the leafhopper can be determined, soon after which the egg turns red as the *A. atomus* develops. When fully mature the parasitized leafhopper egg changes to a darker red/brown colour from which the adult *A. atomus* emerges. The whole life cycle from egg to adult takes some 12–20 days at 25–16°C (77–60°F) respectively.

Crop/pest associations
The parasitoid occurs quite frequently among leafhopper colonies and can build up to high numbers giving a high level of control. However, this usually occurs late in the growing season after considerable damage has been caused by the pest. It should also be remembered that being an egg parasitoid, any unparasitized eggs that survive will pass through all the developmental stages before reaching adulthood to provide the appropriate stage for further parasitism.

Influence on growing practices
Although this organism is being studied currently for its potential as a bio-control agent, little published work appears to have been produced since MacGill (1934). It is known that some chemicals will kill the adults but as all their development occurs within the host egg they are protected from most pesticides. Therefore, short persistence and selective compounds should be safe to integrate with *A. atomus*.

225 *Anagrus atomus* wasps ovipositing in eggs of *Hauptidia maroccana* (glasshouse leafhopper).

226 Eggs of *H. maroccana* parasitized by *A. atomus*.

APHELINUS ABDOMINALIS (DALMAN) (227–230)

Species characteristics
The adult wasp is black and yellow, 1 mm in length and prefers to walk over the crop rather than fly. This habit tends to make the parasitoid remain localized within the crop rather than disperse out. Although it reproduces as a parasitoid, host feeding is an important source of aphid mortality, with each female killing approximately two aphids per day. Parasitized aphids turn black when the parasitoid pupates within the host body and the 'mummified' bodies remain attached to the leaf.

Life cycle
Female *Aphelinus abdominalis* select an aphid of an appropriate size and species before reversing up to it with the ovipositor extended, the tip is inserted into the ventral surface and an egg laid. This hatches within the aphid and the larva feeds on the host's internal tissues; while this proceeds the aphid continues to feed, grow and may produce some offspring before finally being killed as vital body organs are consumed just before parasitoid pupation. At 20°C (68°F) a mummy forms seven days after parasitism, and some 14 days later the adult cuts a circular hole in the aphid and emerges.

Crop/pest associations
The principal host aphids of protected crops are *Macrosiphum euphorbiae* and *Aulacorthum solani* on which *A. abdominalis* prefers to parasitize the second and third instar nymphs. Larger aphids are less frequently attacked, while first and small second instar nymphs are used as food by the adults. Fecundity is low during the first few days of adult life, but by the fourth day may rise to 10–15 eggs/day and, providing host predation continues, does not decline with age. Adult females have a longevity of between 15–27 days and may parasitize over 200 aphids plus also kill 40 or more in the process of host feeding.

Influence on growing practices
A. abdominalis has been recorded as parasitizing a wide range of aphid species in both protected and outdoor crops. Developing wasps still in the aphid skin (mummy stage) are protected from most short persistence insecticides such as fatty acids and plant extract oils that would otherwise kill the adult on contact. Commercial supplies are distributed as black mummies in a vial from which the adults emerge some 2–3 days after receipt; mummies should be placed directly on

the aphid infestation due to host predation by adults wasps. Although they have a wide host range, other parasitoids may be more economic to use against aphids such as *Myzus persicae* and *Aphis gossypii*.

228 An adult *A. abdominalis* among healthy and parasitized *M. euphorbiae*.

229 *A. abdominalis* ovipositing in *M. euphorbiae*.

227 *Macrosiphum euphorbiae* (potato aphids) parasitized by *Aphelinus abdominalis*.

230 *A. abdominalis* ovipositing in *M. euphorbiae*.

APHIDIUS COLEMANI (VIEREK) (231–233)

Species characteristics

Aphidius colemani is a small, black wasp 4–5 mm long that inserts a single egg into a host aphid; all other life stages are within the aphid. The appearance of a golden brown mummy indicates the presence of these parasitoids on a crop. Principal aphids attacked by *A. colemani* include *Aphis gossypii* (melon or cotton aphid), *Myzus persicae* (the peach–potato aphid), and *M. nicotiana* (the tobacco aphid). They are also recorded from other aphids, but less information is available. In general this parasitoid attacks the smaller aphid species.

Life cycle

This life cycle is almost identical to *Aphidius ervi*, except that *A. colemani* has a shorter life cycle (for details see next entry), taking only 14 days at 21°C (70°F) to reach adulthood and approximately 20 days at 15°C (59°F), compared to nearly 19 and 29 days respectively for *A. ervi* at the same temperatures.

Crop/pest associations

Aphidius spp. are good at host location and can provide reasonable levels of control if introduced early when pest numbers are low. However, if aphids are established in colonies, *A. colemani* will take some time to make an impact on the pest population and predators or a selective pesticide should be considered.

Influence on growing practices

Prolonged temperatures above 30°C (86°F) may reduce the efficacy of this parasitoid, particularly on protected crops which should be monitored during hot weather and treated with a compatible insecticide if necessary. The mummy stage is tolerant to most short persistence pesticides but those such as synthetic pyrethroids have long residual activity and may kill the adult as it emerges from the aphid mummy. Banker plants of cereals infested with a specific aphid are useful in crops where a continuous supply of parasitoids is required.

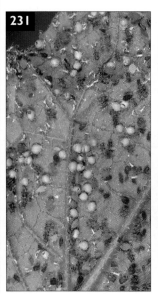

231 Mummies of *Aphis gossypii* (cotton aphid) parasitized by *Aphidius colemani*.

232 Mummies of *A. gossypii* parasitized by *A. colemani*.

233 *A. colemani* wasp ovipositing in *Myzus persicae* (peach–potato aphid).

APHIDIUS ERVI (HALIDAY) (234, 235)

Species characteristics

Aphidius ervi is of European origin, but has been widely introduced to Australia, North and South America and other countries. *A. ervi* tends to parasitize larger aphid species such as *Macrosiphum euphorbiae* (the potato aphid), *Aulacorthum solani* (the glasshouse potato aphid) and *Acyrthosiphon pisum* (the pea aphid) from which it is commonly found. Several other aphid species are also attacked but in commercial use it is targeted at the above named insects. Adults are black and 4–5 mm in length.

Life cycle

In most respects the life cycle of *A. ervi* is very similar to *A. colemani* (see previous entry). The adult female locates a single aphid or a small colony and examines an individual by palpating it with her antennae to determine the size and if it has already been parasitized. If a suitable host is found, the wasp rapidly curls her abdomen under her body and stabs the aphid with her ovipositor to insert an egg that hatches a few days later. The parasitoid larva interferes little with the development or outward appearance of the aphid, except that feeding increases and it secretes more honeydew; they can also produce healthy offspring. When fully developed the parasitoid larva cuts a slit in the underside of the hollowed-out aphid and attaches the carcass to the leaf or other surface including flower, fruit, pot or string. A silken cocoon is spun within the host carcass, which takes on a golden brown colour as the parasitoid pupates and forms the characteristic 'aphid mummy'. After 5–10 days an adult has developed and cuts a circular door in the back of the mummy through which it leaves to seek out new hosts.

Crop/pest associations

Pest control by parasitoids is initially slow, but providing a degree of damage can be tolerated, it is possible to achieve 100% control. Under these conditions swarms of adults can be seen flying close to the tops of plants hunting for aphids to parasitize. A banker plant system may be used to produce high numbers of these parasitoids by infesting cereals with a host plant specific aphid.

Influence on growing practices

A. ervi is active in most crop situations where the above aphids are present, its efficacy may be reduced above 30°C

234 Mummies of *Acrythosiphon pisum* (pea aphid) parasitized by *Aphidius ervi*.

235 *A. ervi* wasp ovipositing in an aphid.

(86°F) and below 8–10°C (46–50°F) although in the mummy stage they are ably to survive frosts. The mummy is also tolerant to most short persistence insecticides (soft soap and natural insecticides) but contact or residual activity of other chemicals can kill adults. *Aphidius* spp. may suffer from hyperparasitoids (a parasitoid of a parasitoid) which can reduce the level of control achieved, particularly late in the season.

COTESIA (=APANTELES) GLOMERATA (LINNAEUS) (236–239)

Species characteristics
Cotesia glomerata adults are about 7 mm in length with long (1.5 mm) upwardly curving antennae. *C. glomerata* is commonly found throughout most of Europe and North America, where it was introduced to control both large and small cabbage white butterfly larvae with great success. The characteristic sulphur-yellow silken cocoons form in irregular masses on almost any surface, from leaves and stems in summer to walls and roofs of buildings during winter.

Life cycle
Females mate immediately after emerging from their pupal cocoon and start egg laying very soon after. Preferring first or young second instar caterpillars (moth larvae), each female can deposit 20–40 eggs per host; a total of up to 200 eggs can be laid per adult. Young *C. glomerata* larvae devour the internal tissues of the living caterpillar and, after 15–20 days when fully developed, they rupture the host body to spill out, forming a mass of individual silken cocoons, often enveloped

by a common web. The life cycle takes 22–30 days from egg to adult depending on temperature; they over-winter within the cocoons, awaiting the next spring before emerging.

Crop/pest associations
Levels of parasitism during early spring are usually low but these can rise to almost 75% by late summer, making an extremely useful contribution to caterpillar control on many brassica crops. *C. glomerata* has been shown to transmit the granulovirus of the small white butterfly, *Pieris rapae*, leading to even higher levels of pest control.

Influence on growing practices
The larvae and adults of most *Cotesia* species are sensitive to pesticides; even Lepidoptera specific products such as *Bacillus thuringiensis* may kill developing larvae unless they can leave the host before it dies. Adult wasps will survive the bacterium provided sufficient healthy hosts also survive. This braconid wasp is not attacked by many hyperparasitoids.

236 Larvae of *Cotesia glomerata* emerging from a parasitized *Pieris brassicae* (cabbage white butterfly) caterpillar.

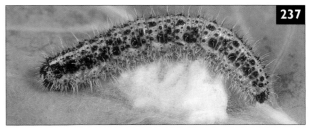

237 Cocoons of *C. glomerata* pupated after leaving a parasitized *P. brassicae* caterpillar.

238 Adult *C. glomerata*.   **239** Adult *C. glomerata*.

DACNUSA SIBIRICA (TELENGER) (240–242)

Species characteristics

Adult *Dacnusa sibirica* are black, 2.5–3 mm in length with long antenna (about the length of the body) and can easily be mistaken for aphid parasitoids (*Aphidius* spp.). This wasp is an endoparasitoid: it lays its egg directly into a young leaf miner larvae without killing it. The parasitoid larva is light grey in colour and curled in a 'C' shape; it develops with the host larva and pupates within the leaf miner puparium.

Life cycle

Host location by the adult parasitoid is initially by scent of the leaf miner frass within the damaged leaf tissue. When a promising leaf has been found the mining larva is located by antennal drumming and a single egg laid inside the host larva which continues to develop through to pupation. The egg and larva of *D. sibirica* can only be found by dissection of the host leaf miner larva. Similarly, during pupation it is difficult to distinguish between healthy and parasitized insects. However, as the parasitoid emerges some 3–5 days before non-parasitized leaf miners, collection of pupae to monitor adult emergence gives a good indication of the parasitoid efficacy.

Crop/pest associations

These commercially available parasitoids work well at low pest densities and may be introduced early in the growing season. They are particularly useful in tomato crops when released during late winter and early spring. As the season progresses and higher numbers of leaf miners may be found, the parasitoid *Diglyphus isaea* is favoured. Use of *D. sibirica* on other commercial crops is dictated by the amount of leaf damage that can be tolerated before adequate control is achieved.

Influence on growing practices

The development time of the parasitoid is some 3–5 days shorter than the host insect and with adult females able to lay over 150 eggs each they can make a reasonable impact on a pest infestation. Temperatures above 22°C (72°F) result in a reduction of egg production. Although *D. sibirica* is a useful and persistent parasitoid against a wide range of leaf miner species it cannot be regarded as a total control agent for leaf miner; that honour falls to *Diglyphus* spp.

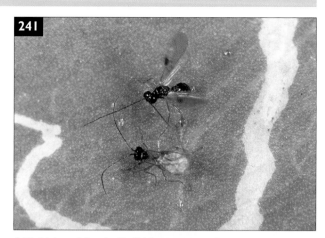

241 Male and female *D. sibirica* wasps courting.

242 *D. sibirica* ovipositing into a leaf miner larva in the leaf mine.

DIADEGMA INSULARE (CRESSON) (243)

Species characteristics

Principally a parasitoid of diamond back moth larvae (*Plutella xylostella*), the ichneumonid wasp *Diadegma insulare* is found throughout Europe and North America. Other species of *Diadegma* may also be found in Asia. Adults are 6 mm long and may be seen roaming over crop foliage searching for host larvae; they are also to be found in or on flowers where they feed on nectar.

Life cycle

Females mate immediately after emerging from their pupal cocoon and then start searching for a suitable young host larva by drumming their antennae. Once located the wasp curls her abdomen under her body and injects a single egg into the moth larva with her ovipositor. The caterpillar is not paralysed and continues to develop through to pupation, at which time the parasitoid exits the host cocoon to spin its own within that of the host. The cycle takes 12–18 days with up to six generations each year. Over-wintering takes place in crop debris as a pupa within the host cocoon.

240 *Phytomyza syngenesiae* (chrysanthemum leaf miner) pupa parasitized by *Dacnusa sibirica*.

243 Female *Diadegma* sp. wasp.

244 *Brevicoryne brassicae* (mealy cabbage aphid) mummies parasitized by *Diaeretiella rapae*, from which one wasp has recently emerged.

Crop/pest associations
As with most parasitoids, activity can be slow during spring but rapidly increases to 70–90% by late summer, providing adequate food sources are available. Due to its widespread habitat *D. insulare* is thought to attack other similar host species of caterpillar that feed on brassica crops.

Influence on growing practices
Adult longevity and fecundity are both increased when nectar is available, as other sources of sugars such as from insect honeydew are reported as inferior to plant nectar. The presence of nectar producing plants either as crops or flowering weeds is thus vitally important to the success of this parasitoid. *D. insulare* adults are susceptible to most insecticides. Developing larvae can also be killed if pesticides, including the Lepidoptera specific *Bacillus thuringiensis*, affect the host caterpillar.

245 *D. rapae* wasp ovipositing in *B. brassicae*.

DIAERETIELLA RAPAE (MCINTOSH) (244, 245)

Species characteristics
A widely distributed parasitoid, *Diaeretiella rapae* is found principally attacking aphids on cabbage, potato and sugar beet, but is also able to parasitize several other species found on related host plants. Adults are 4–5 mm in length, a shiny dark brown colour and may be found feeding on honeydew while they search for aphids. Parasitized aphids take on a light yellowish colour and have a papery appearance to their skin, almost like an inflated paper bag.

Life cycle
Single aphids or small colonies are located by female *D. rapae*. Individual aphids are examined by antennal palpation to determine size and evidence of previous parasitization. After a suitable host has been selected, the female curls her abdomen under her body and holding the aphid with her antennae, an egg is inserted which hatches after a few days. The parasitized aphid continues to develop quite normally except that slightly more honeydew is produced. When the parasitoid larva is fully developed it cuts a slit along the underside of the now empty aphid body and attaches the carcass to the leaf or other surface by spinning a silken cocoon in which it pupates. After 6–12 days the adult has developed within the mummy, and cuts an almost circular door in the back of the aphid through which it leaves.

Crop/pest associations
Three or more generations of parasitoids may occur each year and a considerable number of aphids parasitized. However, due to the dense colonies of aphids such as *Brevicoryne brassicae*, effective control is rarely achieved. Higher numbers of parasitoids have been found when areas around cultivated fields have been allowed to grow a variety of wild plants such as *Chenopodium* (fat hen), thistles, and brassica plants.

Influence on growing practices
D. rapae is sensitive to many pesticides used in commercial agriculture, and their numbers may be depleted in areas of intensive cropping. The use of selective pesticides compatible with ICM techniques helps to increase parasitoid populations. Unfortunately this may have detrimental effect when marketing a crop due to high numbers of mummies on plants, as happened in the UK in 1998 resulting in many cauliflower heads being down-graded.

DIGLYPHUS ISAEA (WALKER) (246–250)

Species characteristics

This is an ectoparasitoid: one that paralyses its host before laying one or more eggs next to the larva. Adults are small and vary in length from 1–2.3 mm; they have a black background colour with a metallic green sheen, and females have a yellow stripe on the hind leg. *D. isaea* is common throughout the summer on leaf miner infested weeds, particularly milk thistles which can produce up to 80 parasitoids per plant, making them worth collecting to harvest the parasitoids.

Life cycle

Adult females generally attack second instar leaf miner larva (mines approximately 2 cm in length), host location is by antennal drumming and the scent produced by the feeding leaf miner. Once a suitable host has been found the wasp stings the larva, permanently paralysing it before depositing 1–3 eggs immediately next to it. The parasitoid larvae plug into their host and develop a blue green colour as they reach maturity. When fully grown the parasitoid larvae move away from the dead host and collect frass pellets which are placed one above the other to produce miniature 'pit props'. These prevent damage to the pupae as they develop to adulthood before emerging from the leaf through a hole in the epidermis.

Crop/pest associations

These commercially available parasitoids work better at high or increasing pest densities and may be introduced when leaf miner numbers reach one new mine per plant per week. They are particularly useful in tomato crops when released during early spring. The parasitoid requires sunny conditions for maximum activity and frequently produces more than one parasitoid from each host larva; where multi-parasitism occurs the resulting adults vary greatly in size. *D. isaea* usually kill more leaf miners by stinging and feeding on the wound than by parasitism, particularly when the wasps are young and eggs are still developing. The ability of *D. isaea* to multiply rapidly and to hyperparasitize *Dacnusa sibirica* and other leaf miner parasitoids usually makes it the dominant species of leaf miner parasitoid during summer months.

Influence on growing practices

Under conditions of low light, too few leaf miner or hosts of the wrong age range *D. isaea* may be slow to exert its full control potential. However, once fully established in a crop the results can be spectacular by a combination of multi-parasitism and host feeding by adult wasps on mining larvae. Although most acaricides and fungicides can be integrated with these parasitoids, it is thought the use of sulphur either as a fumigant or spray against powdery mildew disrupts host location by the parasitoid.

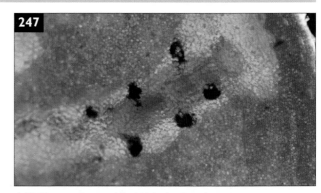

247 'Pit props' created by *Diglyphus isaea* larvae.

248 *D. isaea* pupa within the leaf mine.

249 *D. isaea* wasps investigating suitable host leaf miner larvae.

246 *Diglyphus isaea* wasp larva developing from an egg laid outside the leaf miner larva.

250 *D. isaea* adult ovipositing in a leaf miner larva.

ENCARSIA FORMOSA (GAHAN) (251–254)

Species characteristics

The whitefly parasitoid *Encarsia formosa* was found in England and successfully used first in 1926. Within two years 250,000 parasitoids had been reared and sent around England and then on to Canada. Adult females are 0.6 mm long with a black head and thorax, a yellow abdomen and translucent wings. *E. formosa* males are of similar size to females, but are all black and usually only make up about 1–2% of the population; they may be produced when a second egg is laid into a host already parasitized by *E. formosa*. This is known as auto-parasitism or multi-parasitism and occurs most frequently at very high temperatures. The most obvious sign of *Encarsia* spp. activity is the presence of black scales on leaves; these are the pupal stage of the parasitoid and are formed inside the pupae of the whitefly.

Life cycle

Adult wasps are attracted to the host whitefly scale (so called because the larval stage of whitefly is mostly immobile and resembles miniature scale insects) by volatile compounds given off from whitefly honeydew. Adults feed on honeydew and also from wounds to the whitefly larvae made by oviposition; this can kill some scales so neither whitefly or parasitoid develops. Usually a single egg is laid which passes through three larval stages, during which time the whitefly scale remains white and develops normally. When fully developed (about ten days after oviposition at 22°C [72°F]) the whitefly scale turns black as the parasitoid pupates. The pupae remain attached to the leaf and the adult emerges some ten days later from a hole cut through the puparium with a special 'tooth'.

Crop/pest associations

E. formosa is introduced to crops as black scales from which adults emerge a few days later. The safe emergence of this parasitoid is characterized by a 'D'-shaped exit hole in the top of the scale, which can clearly be seen by shining a light through. Under ideal conditions up to a total of 300 eggs can be laid at a rate of approximately 12–15 per day. The structure of the host plant influences *E. formosa* parasitism: cucumber has hairy leaves which trap whitefly honeydew making mobility difficult, whereas this occurs much less on aubergine, tomato and most ornamentals.

Influence on growing practices

E. formosa is commercially available throughout the year, but is most active at above 18°C (64°F) with good light intensity. Long periods of poor light and cooler conditions disrupt its activity and can allow the whitefly to get troublesome. Adult whitefly lay their eggs on the apical leaves, and as the plant continues growing upwards the developing scales tend to be lower down the plant. On crops such as tomato, where the lower leaves are regularly removed to allow light and access to the fruit for picking, de-leafing too high up the plant can deplete the parasitoid black scales before they emerge.

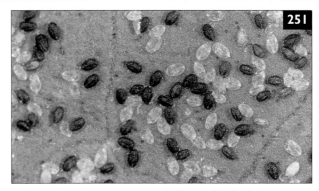

251 *Trialeurodes vaporariorum* (glasshouse whitefly) larvae and pupae parasitized by *Encarsia formosa*.

252 *E. formosa* adult wasp emerging from a parasitized *T. vaporariorum* pupa.

253 *E. formosa* adult wasp with parasitized *T. vaporariorum* larvae and pupae.

254 *E. formosa* adult wasp with *T. vaporariorum* scales and pupae.

ERETMOCERUS EREMICUS (ROSE AND ZOLNEROWICH) (255–258)

Species characteristics
Eretmocerus eremicus is a small (0.5–0.6 mm) parasitoid wasp that attacks the larval stages of whitefly, in particular *Trialeurodes vaporariorum* (the glasshouse whitefly) and *Bemisia tabaci* (the sweet potato whitefly). The latter species has a notifiable status in several countries due to its potential to transmit many plant viruses to a wide range of both edible and ornamental crops. *E. eremicus* originates from the deserts of Arizona and California where it tolerates extremes of temperature of almost freezing to over 40°C (104°F).

Life cycle
Female parasitoids deposit a single egg under the whitefly larval scale that, on hatching, burrows into the host where a protective capsule is formed around the developing parasitoid. Although eggs can be laid beneath any of the larval instars there is a preference for the second instar. Successful parasitism is evident by the yellow colour and visible presence of a parasitoid body, particularly when close to emergence when the adult can be clearly seen. At an average temperature of 23°C (74°F) parasitoid development from egg to adult takes 17–18 days, with the pupal stage occupying up to eight days of this time. The life cycle slows at lower temperatures, taking some 40 days at 17°C (63°F).

Crop/pest associations
Eretmocerus spp. are becoming extremely useful for whitefly control when continuous high temperatures adversely affect *Encarsia formosa*, and also for crops where there is a threat or presence of *Bemisia tabaci*. Adult wasps are introduced to the crop at rates of up to 20/m² in areas of heavy whitefly infestation for up to six weeks, or until adequate control is achieved. Where pest levels are lower or additional control is being used, rates of 3–5/m² will provide reasonable protection from the major whitefly species.

Influence on growing practices
Although the wasp is not as efficient as *Encarsia formosa* in terms of parasitoid reproduction, *E. eremicus* can result in equally high numbers of whitefly mortality due to host feeding. The overall result is comparable in terms of pest control for temperate environments, but exceeds *E. formosa* where high temperatures and low humidities are prevalent.

256 *T. vaporariorum* scales and pupae parasitized by *E. eremicus*.

257 Adult *E. eremicus* with *T. vaporariorum* pupa.

255 Adult *Eretmocerus eremicus* wasps with parasitized *Trialeurodes vaporariorum* scales and pupae.

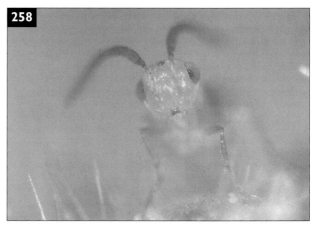

258 Head-on view of *E. eremicus*.

LEPTOMASTIX DACTYLOPII (WALKER) (259, 260)
LEPTOMASTIX EPONA (WALKER)

Species characteristics

These small (about 3 mm long) parasitoid wasps are a useful addition to the control of the mealybug *Planoccus citri* and *Pseudococcus viburni* (Signoret) (the citrus and glasshouse mealybugs respectively). *L. dactylopii* is yellowish-brown in colour with relatively long, hinged antenna which it taps to locate the host. *L. epona* is more uniformly dark brown in colour. Adult wasps are good fliers and with their hopping flight can provide excellent control of mealybugs even when the host is at low density.

Life cycle

The female lays between 80 and 100 eggs, singly into third instar and adult mealybugs. The developing wasp larva feeds on the host body fluids, consuming the majority of the mealybug. Where the host provides insufficient nutrition due to its size or age, male parasitoids are usually formed, but in general the sex ratio is 1:1 with unmated females producing only male offspring. Pupation occurs within the mummified skin of the host, which resembles a slightly bulbous body covered with fine threads. When fully developed the parasitoid cuts a hinged lid through the mealybug skin and pushes its way out. Egg to adult development takes 3–4 weeks depending on temperature.

259 *Leptomastix dactylopii* wasp.

Crop/pest associations

L. dactylopii is specific against *P. citri*, which can be identified by its very short tail filaments, while *L. epona* will attack *P. viburni* and *P. maritimus* (Erhorn) that have tail filaments approximately one-third of the body length. Releases of up to 2/m² of planted area or five per infested plant are usually adequate if started in late spring, with a single repeat some 3–4 weeks later. The parasitoids will remain active up to the early autumn period when cooler, dull conditions curtail their activities and control ceases. However, under summer conditions they are capable of providing up to 90% parasitism of low level infestations on some plants, providing humidity levels are not excessively low.

Influence on growing practices

Commercial supplies of these parasitoids are frequently erratic in some European countries and their availability is limited to their seasonal activity, although re-establishment from one year's introduction to the next year is common. It should also be remembered that the parasitoid is principally used in conjunction with the far more polyphagous predator *Cryptolaemus montrouzieri* that is more effective against large infestations of mealybugs.

260 *L. dactylopii* wasp with *Planococcus citri* (citrus mealybugs).

METAPHYCUS HELVOLUS (COMPERE) (261)

Species characteristics
These small (1.5–2.0 mm) wasps are parasitoids of various soft scale insects; females are orange-yellow and males dark brown. Native to South Africa, they have been introduced to almost all semi-tropical areas to control soft black scale (*Saisettia oleae* [Bernard]) on citrus and olive. They are also routinely introduced to interior atriums and conservatories for control of several species of soft scale. In temperate climates their season of activity is likely to be restricted to the summer months, although small populations can over-winter to reappear the following year. Adults are relatively long-lived at 2.5–3 months, providing an adequate food source of honeydew and young scale insects are available for host feeding.

Life cycle
Each female lays an average of 400 eggs at up to five per day, usually in late second or third instar nymphs. The eggs hatch after a couple of days to minute larvae that develop, singly, within the scale insects body, turning it a darker brown to black colour as the parasitoid matures. After 11–12 days at 30°C (86°F) the adult emerges through a small hole cut through the top of the scale, females being produced in larger hosts and males in smaller ones.

Crop/pest associations
Control of brown soft scale (*Coccus hesperidum* [Linnaeus]) may be less effective by *M. helvolus* due to encapsulation of eggs and young larvae within the host body. Temperatures above 30°C (86°F) also tend to increase the level of encapsulation. However, at higher temperatures there is a marked increase in searching efficiency, egg production and host feeding that can account for greater pest mortality than by parasitism alone.

Influences on growing practices
Under normal growing conditions on open field crops, scale insects are rarely a major pest problem. However, these parasitoids are relatively delicate and their level of control may be disrupted by several factors including dust on leaves that can raise the leaf temperature and from chemical residues. Pesticide sprays, usually targeted at other pests, can interfere with *Metaphycus* spp. causing an increase in scale insects, which in turn can require more sprays to correct the in-balance between pest and natural enemy.

PRAON MYZIPHAGUM (MACKAUER) (262, 263) PRAON VOLUCRE (HALIDAY)

Species characteristics
Praon myziphagum and *P. volucre* are polyphagous parasitoids that frequently attack winged aphids, which in turn carry the immature parasitoid long distances during their migratory flights. Adults are 2.5–3 mm in length with a shiny black head and thorax, brown abdomen and legs. *Praon* spp. are distinctive in that the last larval instar and pupa are in a silvery-tan silk pad spun beneath the mummified body of the host aphid. Adults feed on honeydew and are not recorded as killing aphids by host feeding.

Life cycle
Female *Praon* spp. lay most of their eggs within the first 4–5 days after emergence. They select suitable second and third stage nymph aphids with their antennae and, once located, insert a single egg that hatches after 3–4 days. Parasitized aphids continue to develop and on reaching maturity can reproduce until quite late in the parasitoid's life cycle. The last larval instar cuts a slit in the underside of the host and spins a double-walled silken cocoon that raises the aphid body off the leaf surface. Adult emergence occurs after 2–3 weeks at 16–24°C (61–75°F) when a small exit hole is bitten through the side of the raised silken cocoon.

Crop/pest associations
Praon spp. are commonly found in the spring as the first naturally occurring aphid parasitoids; their wide host range makes them useful for inoculative introductions on most crops. As with other aphid parasitoids, initial control may be slow to achieve but their presence is usually welcome.

Influence on growing practices
For successful adult emergence a reasonably high humidity is required (average protected cropping conditions seem to be adequate), which may preclude their use in interior landscaping. The presence of too many silvery mummies on leaves of ornamentals may affect the quality appearance of the product. Parasitoids within the mummy cocoon are tolerant to most short persistence pesticides but can killed by broad-spectrum and long persistence insecticides.

261 *Metaphycus helvolus.*

262 *Praon* sp. wasp cocoon developed outside an alate aphid.

263 *Praon myziphagum* wasp.

264 Lepidoptera eggs parasitized by *Trichogramma* sp. wasp.

TRICHOGRAMMA SPP. (264–266)

Species characteristics
There are many species of trichogrammatid parasitoids found throughout the world. These minute wasps (less than 1 mm in length) feed on and parasitize the eggs of Lepidoptera and occasionally Coleoptera and Hymenoptera. The first mass production of a *Trichogramma* species was in 1926, when 200,000 adult parasitoids were released in walnut orchards against codling moth in Ventura County, southern California. However, most research and practical use of these parasitoids occurs in China, North American forest systems, the Soviet Union and western Europe, where they are routinely used on forestry and arable systems. This makes them the most widely studied of all biological control agents in the world.

Life cycle
Adult parasitoids locate moth eggs by the kairomones produced and left by their hosts. Once a suitable egg has been found, the wasp drills into it with her ovipositor and lays one or more eggs, depending on size. The larva has three instars and pupates inside the host egg, turning it black and killing it. Development of *Trichogramma* spp. ceases below 10°C (50°F) and the parasitoid can diapause within the host egg.

265 *Trichogramma* sp. wasp with *Sitotroga cerealella* eggs.

Crop/pest associations
Commercial production is commonly performed on the eggs of corn moths *Ephestia kuehniella*, and *Sitotroga cerealella*. A useful semi-artificial diet has also been developed by the Chinese. Moth eggs used for mass-rearing are killed by ultra violet radiation or freezing before parasitism, to ensure no pest species are introduced.

Influence on growing practices
Trichogramma spp. generally show poor ability to disperse from release sites. To overcome this problem very high numbers are used (75,000/hectare/week for protected crops and up to several million per hectare seasonally for open crops), and repeated releases are performed through the risk periods. Parasitized host eggs may be glued to small cards for distribution by hand to ground crops or distributed by plane or helicopter for large field crops, orchards and forests. Supplementary treatments with selective insecticides or the bacterium *Bacillus thuringiensis* may be necessary for control of any surviving caterpillars not killed as moth eggs.

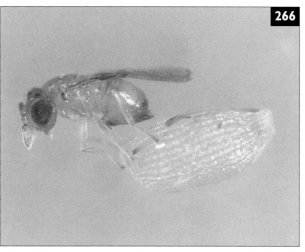

266 *Trichogramma* sp. wasp about to oviposit in a *S. cerealella* egg.

Neuroptera

Adult neuropterans are either predatory or omnivorous, feeding on fungal hyphae, pollen and honeydew. Adults of the genus *Chrysoperla* belong to the second group and feed only on honeydew and pollen. To overcome any dietary shortages of essential amino acids they have a symbiotic yeast (*Torulopsis* spp.) living around their mouth-parts (**267**). Although some species are specialist feeders, the larvae of most species are regarded as generalist predators, feeding with formidable looking mouth-parts that both pierce and suck the body juices of its prey. The digestive system of lacewing larva has no direct passage to the anus. Instead the small amount of solid material ingested accumulates within the gut and is voided when it reaches adulthood. This is due to the mainly liquid diet of lacewing larvae. *Chrysoperla* spp. are easier to mass rear than *Chrysopa* spp., consequently more research work has been done on the former genus. Adult *Chrysoperla* spp. can also be attracted to crops before pest numbers become excessive by spraying honeydew, sucrose solution or molasses over the plants. Some less common lacewing adults are shown in (**268**, **269**).

267 Predatory mouth-parts of *Chrysopa perla* (lacewing).

268 *Hemorobius humulinus* (brown lacewing) adult.

269 *Raphidia* sp. (snake fly).

CHRYSOPA PERLA (LINNAEUS) (270, 271)

Species characteristics
Similar and often confused with *Chrysoperla carnea*, the adults of the *Chrysopa* genus are all predatory, feeding on a range of soft-bodied prey. *C. perla* adults are 15–20 mm in length with their wings folded and have a wing span of up to 30 mm. They are commonly found across northern Europe and, rarely, in the hotter areas of the Mediterranean region or much of Asia.

Life cycle
Blue/green eggs are laid at the end of a mucus stalk up to 5 mm in length, deposited either singly or several may be found close together, depending mainly on the quantity of available food for the larvae. Mature larvae spin a silken cocoon in which they pupate and from which they emerge as adults. *C. perla* over-winter (diapause) as larvae in cocoons and continue development as conditions warm the following spring.

Crop/pest associations
Although regarded as generalist predators, research has shown that a diet of certain aphids alone will allow full development through to adulthood, but can result in reduced viability of the adult insect. As with other lacewings, the adults prefer an open plant structure to fly through, but the larvae tend to be found hidden within a leaf canopy.

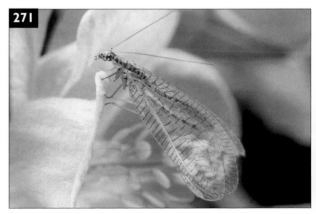

270 *Chrysopa perla* larva feeding on *Myzus persicae* (peach–potato aphid).

271 *C. perla* adult.

Influence on growing practices
The mass production of *Chrysopa* spp. is more complicated than that of *Chrysoperla* spp., consequently most lacewings purchased for commercial use are *Chrysoperla carnea*. Nevertheless, *C. perla* are widely used in several countries alongside other beneficial organisms to control aphids on many crops. They may be introduced as young larvae or commonly as eggs.

272 *Chrysoperla carnea* empty egg attached to an apple leaf.

CHRYSOPERLA CARNEA (STEPHENS) (272–275)

Species characteristics
Known as common green lacewings after the delicate wing venation of adults, or the aphid lion after the voracious appetite of its larvae, *Chrysoperla carnea* is an active predator of many soft-bodied arthropods and their eggs. The genus *Chrysoperla* is comprized of a complex of closely related species, many of which have been well studied throughout the world. Various species are mass-produced in several countries for use on both outdoor and protected crops, e.g. the closely related *C. rufilabris* is often commercially used in North America. Adults are 12–20 mm long with a wingspan of up to 30 mm and have long antennae and bright golden eyes. Mature larvae are 10 mm in length.

273 *C. carnea* larva attacking *Macrosiphum rosae* (Linnaeus) (rose aphids).

Life cycle
The optimum conditions for *C. carnea* reproduction are 20°C (68°F) and 80% humidity, with a day length of 15–17 hours. Blue/green eggs are laid supported on mucus stalks 4–5 mm long on leaves or plant stems close to their host food. These hatch after 3–5 days to produce tiny active predators that feed on honeydew, insect eggs or small prey. The third instar larva is extremely voracious and can consume a whitefly pupae in less than one minute. The larvae are cannibals which, when young, may eat unhatched eggs, other larvae and even adults if food becomes scarce. A silken white cocoon is produced from which the adult emerges and invariably flies away giving little contribution to localized pest control. Over-wintering adults turn a pink to brown colour and frequently seek refuge in buildings or leaf litter. Special boxes are available to encourage adults to remain within a local area.

274 *C. carnea* adult.

Crop/pest associations
In the presence of mixed prey, green lacewings attack aphids first, followed by thrips and spider mites. They are also known to feed well on young caterpillar and moth eggs, mealybugs, scale insects, whitefly larvae and pupae. Plants with dense foliage are best suited to these predators, particularly when there is an even spread of prey through the canopy. Frequently in these situations parasitoids are much less effective and chrysopids have a niche environment.

Influence on growing practices
Due to mass-production systems, lacewing larvae are becoming more widely used on a range of crops to control different pests on plants growing in many environments, including interior atriums, field, garden, orchard and protected crops. They are useful on organic crops where pesticide restrictions necessitate a more generalist predator to control many pest species. *C. carnea* are more tolerant to low humidities than other lacewing species.

275 *C. carnea* adult with diapausal colouration.

Arachnidae

SPIDERS (PAGE 94)
HARVESTMEN (PAGE 98)
PREDATORY MITES (PAGE 99)

Spiders are present as polyphagous predators in virtually all crop and garden situations (**276–279**). They can be extremely numerous but often go unnoticed because of their size and relatively secretive habits. Different spider families have different techniques for catching their prey, with some spinning webs and others jumping or running. Most will bite if handled roughly, but few are venomous to mammals.

Spiders can be recognized by the fact that their body is divided into two parts, a cephalothorax and an abdomen, and by the presence of eight legs. Spiders have six or (more typically) eight eyes. The relative position of the eyes is widely used in the classification of spiders.

Spiders are difficult to identify readily in the field and it is often necessary to examine them with a hand lens or a binocular microscope to identify them more than at family level. Male spiders are typically identified by the shape of their palps, whereas females are normally identified by their epigynes (the female genital area on the underside of the abdomen). Colour and size are not always reliable features when identifying spiders.

276 A spider on a dew-covered barley leaf in the early morning sun.

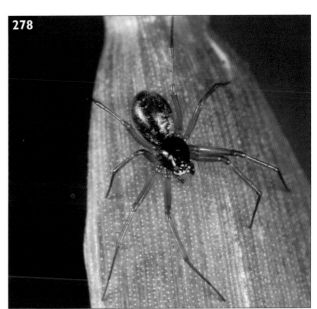

278 A linyphiid spider *Lepthyphantes tenuis* (Blackwall).

277 *Trochosa* sp. hunting spider with an egg sac.

279 An orb-web spider *Araneus diadematus* (Clerck) (garden spider).

ARANEIDAE (280, 281)

Species characteristics

Spiders of the family Araneidae have relatively poor eyesight and are all spinners of orb-shaped webs. Araneidae are usually seen sitting on or to one side of the web. They detect the presence of prey in the web by vibration. When prey is caught in the web it is wrapped in silk before being bitten. One of the most common araneid species in fruit orchards, *Araniella cucurbitina* (Clerck) has a bright green abdomen with paired black spots. The females are 4–6 mm in length and the males are 3.5–4 mm in length.

Life cycle

The life cycles of the Araneidae are diverse, even within a genus.

Crop/pest associations

Araneid spiders feed on insects which fly into their webs. In fruit orchards these may include pest species such as aphids or psyllids. Because they are polyphagous and are not restricted to a particular prey type, spiders can survive in crops with no pest species present.

Influence on growing practices

Members of the genus *Araniella* are common in apple and pear orchards and have been shown to be more abundant where flowering strips are also present. The flowering plants attract a wide range of flying insect species, many of which are trapped in the webs of *Araniella* spp. Orchards planted with flowering strips have been shown to have fewer aphids where higher numbers of *Araniella* spp. were observed. Because web-spinning spiders may re-use their webs they can receive high oral doses of pesticide treatments and therefore may be more sensitive than other spiders. Pyrethroid insecticides are particularly damaging to araneid spiders.

280 *A. diadematus* on a dew-covered web in the early morning.

281 *A. diadematus* head-on view of male spider showing the eyes and palps.

LINYPHIIDAE (282–285)

Species characteristics
One of the largest families of spiders, the Linyphiidae are also the most numerous in gardens and agricultural crops. Linyphiid spiders are difficult to identify since they are classified by the absence of the characteristics of other spider families. Plainly marked Linyphiidae are known as money spiders and were considered to bring good fortune. The commonest genera in agricultural crops include *Erigone*, *Oedothorax* and *Lepthyphantes*. Linyphiidae range in size from 1–5.5 mm.

Life cycle
Eggs are laid in egg sacs on the underside of leaves or under stones. Linyphiid spiders construct webs with no refuge and are often seen on the underside of their webs. In late summer and early autumn linyphiid spiders can be found 'ballooning', dispersing on threads of silk and being blown on currents of warm air.

Crop/pest associations
Linyphiid spiders are polyphagous predators in all crops and gardens and consume aphids and other invertebrate prey.

Influence on growing practices
Linyphiidae are very numerous in most crops and gardens and spin webs at different heights within the canopy. Aphids, which regularly fall from the plant to the ground, can be caught in linyphiid webs, as can smaller flying insects.

282 *Erigone* sp. (money spider) adult.

283 *Erigone atra* adult female.

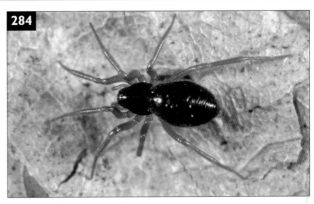

284 *Oedothorax retusus* (Westring) adult.

285 *Lepthyphantes tenuis* adult.

LYCOSIDAE (WOLF SPIDERS) (286–288)

Species characteristics
The commonest large spiders found on the ground in most agricultural crops, Lycosidae are identified by the position of their eyes. The front of the carapace has a row of four small eyes, evenly spaced. Above them are a pair of larger forward facing eyes. Further back on the carapace are a second pair of large eyes. A line through the outer large eyes will meet the mid line of the spider in front of the carapace. Lycosidae are generally brown in colour with markings on the carapace and abdomen and with a dense covering of hairs. Some spiders are active at night but many are also seen on warm sunny days running on the soil surface. Species are identified by examination of the palps of males and the epigynes of the females.

Life cycle
From early summer onwards female lycosid spiders begin to carry a conspicuous pale coloured egg sac attached to their abdomen. After 2–3 weeks the eggs hatch and the young spiderlings are carried by the female for up to one week. Females may make up to three eggs sacs in a season. Males generally die in mid summer.

Crop/pest associations
Lycosidae are hunting spiders and will feed on a variety of small insects or mites in most crop situations. They feed readily on aphids on the ground but do not actively climb the plants in search of prey. In cereal crops spiders of the genus *Pardosa* are particularly common and are voracious polyphagous predators.

Influence on growing practices
Lycosidae like shelter and high humidity and are less abundant in open dry habitats. Provision of beetle banks would also enhance wolf spider numbers. Lycosidae are sensitive to insecticides, particularly organophosphates and pyrethroids.

286 *Pisaura mirabilis* (Clerck) (hunting spider) on a wheat ear.

SALTICIDAE (289)

Species characteristics
Salticids are hunting spiders with very good eyesight. Salticids have a characteristic square-fronted carapace with four large forward facing eyes on the front, a smaller pair slightly further back and a larger pair further back still. If an object enters their field of vision salticid spiders will jump round to focus the large front eyes on it. Salticids are often covered in hairs which may be brightly iridescent or dark. Salticids do not spin webs and several species are thought to mimic ants. These cosmopolitan salticids are sometimes called jumping spiders, since they stalk their prey, often jumping to capture it.

Life cycle
The life cycles of salticid spiders are diverse, even within a genus.

Crop/pest associations
Salticid spiders are polyphagous predators, consuming a wide range of insect prey in almost every crop system. Salticids will prefer ground cover and are often seen running through grass and low vegetation. Some species are also active on tree trunks.

Influence on growing practices
Salticid spiders are unlikely to be active in areas with bare soil, for example on herbicide-treated strips beneath orchard trees. All spiders are more abundant in unsprayed crops and are particularly susceptible to pyrethroid insecticides.

287 *P. mirabilis* (hunting spider) with an egg sac.

288 *Pardosa* sp. (wolf spider) with an egg sac.

289 *Salticus scenicus* (Clerck) (zebra jumping spider).

THOMISIDAE (290, 291)

Species characteristics
Thomisid spiders, also known as crab spiders, have the front two pairs of legs longer than the back two pairs and usually adopt a characteristic crab-like stance. These spiders can move sideways like a crab, as well as forwards and backwards. There can be considerable colour variation within species of Thomisidae and they are often coloured to match their surroundings. Thomisidae do not spin webs but catch their prey by waiting camouflaged in flowers or on leaves with their front legs held open. When an insect ventures near enough the spider pounces and seizes its prey. *Xysticus cristatus* is the most common thomisid spider found on trees and bushes and has a pattern of stacked triangles on its abdomen. Adult thomisid spiders typically have body lengths of between 4–8 mm.

Life cycle
Thomisid spiders have varied life cycles, even within a genus.

Crop/pest associations
Thomisidae are common as predators in fruit crops, particularly in warmer climates. Since they are polyphagous they feed on a variety of arthropod species which may include insect pests. Thomisidae are particularly noticeable when there are large numbers of flying insects in a crop, for example at the time of flowering in fruit trees.

Influence on growing practices
Like all spiders Thomisidae are extremely sensitive to pyrethroid insecticides but are probably not harmed by most fungicide treatments.

290 *Misumena vatia* (Clerck) (crab spider) in an umbellifer flower.

291 *M. vatia* attacking a bumble bee from a betony flower (photograph courtesy of Phil McLean/Holt Studios).

Opiliones HARVESTMEN

PHALANGIUM OPILIO (LINNAEUS) (292–294)

Species characteristics
Harvestmen such as *Phalangium opilio* have four pairs of legs which are unusually long in relation to their body. The body (4.0–9.0 mm in length) when viewed from above is oval in shape and gives the impression of being a single segment (although it is in fact two). The abdomen is further segmented whereas in spiders there is no abdominal segmentation. Harvestmen have two sideways facing eyes, which in most families are mounted on a central raised structure, an ocularium. Females are larger than males.

Life cycle
Eggs are laid in batches in soil or other damp medium during the late summer and autumn and hatch in the spring. Juvenile harvestmen pass through up to eight instars throughout spring and summer and reach sexual maturity in late summer. Harvestmen are most abundant in mid summer. Adults and juveniles of *P. opilio* can also over-winter.

Crop/pest associations
Harvestmen are predators and occur in most crop and garden habitats where there is high humidity. *P. opilio* is found throughout the Palearctic, North America and New Zealand where it is found in disturbed habitats in grass and surface litter. Harvestmen will attach to any available soft-bodied insects including aphids.

Influence on growing practices
Harvestmen cannot tolerate dry conditions and prefer ground close to water or shelter. Grassy banks at field margins will encourage harvestmen, as will dense undergrowth and hedgerows.

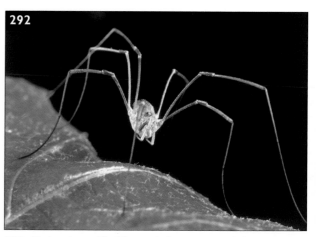

292 *Phalangium opilio* (Linnaeus) (harvestman) adult (note that harvestmen commonly lose one or more legs).

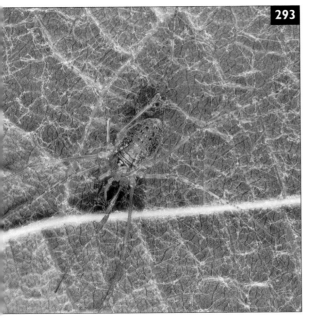

293 *Phalangium* sp. immature harvestman.

294 *Leiobunum rotundum* adult.

Acari

Acari are small, fast moving mites that can be specific predators as with *Phytoseiulus persimilis* (**295**), or more generalist in their diet as are many of the *Neoseiulus* species. The generic names of this group are under revision and their name can change as taxonomists work through these predatory mites. All deposit eggs close to the intended prey that hatch as six-legged nymphs, pass through two moults and develop as eight-legged adults. Location of prey is usually by kairomone released by the prey faeces, plant damage, or, in the case of spider mites, by their webbing that produces an attractant and arrestment stimulus in the predator. Most predatory mites are capable of surviving on relatively low numbers of prey and can increase rapidly and provide adequate levels of control before any major outbreak occurs. Predatory mites are found throughout the world and several are in commercial production for mass release to many crops, particularly fruit such as strawberries that receive a premium if not sprayed during harvest.

295 *Phytoseiulus persimilis* adult feeding on a *Tetranychus urticae* (2-spotted spider mite) egg. The larger egg belongs to *P. persimilis*.

ALLOTHROMBIDIUM SPP. (296, 297)

Species characteristics

Commonly known as red velvet mites due to the high levels of carotene giving the bright red colour and the velvet coat of fine hairs covering their bodies, *Allothrombidium* spp. are the largest of the mite family (Trombidiidae). Adult females are 4 mm in length and become more noticeable under hot dry conditions, when adults run freely over the ground, including stone and concrete surfaces. Velvet mites are common throughout temperate regions; tropical species of giant red velvet mites can reach 10–12 mm x 6–8 mm across and are specialized predators of termites.

Life cycle

Allothrombidium spp. have one generation each year and spend most of their life underground, only venturing out during warm dry periods. Small orange coloured eggs, 0.2 mm in diameter are deposited in crevices below the ground and hatch to a six-legged larva that attaches itself to a host prey. After its first moult the larva gains another pair of legs to form an eight-legged nymph.

Crop/pest associations

The larvae are ectoparasitoids and feed on many hosts including insects and other mites. Adults and nymphs are predatory and are frequently found amongst aphid colonies, where they may kill several individuals per day.

296 *Allothrombidium fuliginosum* (velvet mite) parasitic nymph stage attached to an aphid *Macrosiphum* sp.

297 *A. fuliginosum* adult.

Influence on growing practices

Larvae and nymphs feeding on aphids and other prey are susceptible to pesticide sprays; frequently cultivated ground can also upset their breeding sites. Red velvet mites are thought to have few natural enemies.

AMBLYSEIUS (NEOSEIULUS) CALIFORNICUS (MCGREGOR) (298)

Species characteristics

Amblyseius californicus is a predatory mite specialized in feeding on spider mites, including *Panonychus ulmi* (fruit tree spider mite), *Tetranychus urticae* (glasshouse spider mite) and *T. cinabarinus* (carmine spider mite). Adults are 1.25 mm in length and can produce over 60 eggs per female. They can also feed on other arthropod prey and pollen when the favoured food is scarce; this allows better survival than many obligate predators.

Life cycle

Adult females attach their eggs singly to leaf hairs along veins on the underside of leaves close to spider mite colonies; these hatch to a six-legged larva, which develops through to protonymph and deutonymphal stages before reaching adulthood. This takes almost ten days at 21°C (70°F) but only five days at 30°C (86°F), which is marginally quicker than its principal prey *T. urticae*.

Crop/pest associations

Studies on Californian strawberries indicate that *A. californicus* is a less effective predator than *Phytoseiulus persimilis* as fewer eggs are laid, it has a lower rate of population growth, searching for prey is less thorough and fewer prey are consumed. However, it is reported from various glasshouses and field crops to persist for longer and to control spider mites in situations where *P. persimilis* is not so effective. These include hot, dry environments and ornamental or foliage plants where spider mite densities may be low.

Influence on growing practices

A. californicus is reported as being highly tolerant to several of the more commonly used pesticides from the organophosphate, carbamate, and synthetic pyrethroid groups. In any environment where predators are being used it is always advisable to use selective or compatible pesticides should they be necessary. Due to their slower rate of activity, a selective acaricide may be necessary to reduce plant damage before the predator gives adequate levels of control.

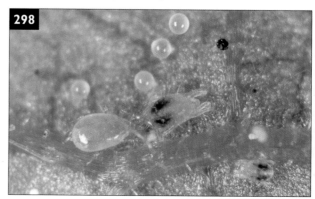

298 *Amblyseius californicus* adult mite attacking *Tetranychus urticae* (2-spotted spider mite).

AMBLYSEIUS (NEOSEIULUS) CUCUMERIS (OUDEMANS) (299)

Species characteristics
Amblyseius cucumeris is a predatory mite and one of a group of thrips feeders, 1.25 mm in length and pale in colour. Nymphs and adults have eight legs and use the front pair as feelers. They are polyphagous predators and although naturally occurring in many crops throughout the temperate regions, it is their commercialization that has spread their range.

Life cycle
The oval eggs (about 0.14 mm diameter) are deposited on pubescent hairs of the mid vein axil, and similarly on the lateral veins on the underside of leaves. They are translucent pink/white in colour. On hatching the larva have six legs and do not feed for several hours. The two nymphal stages both have eight legs, are very mobile and active feeders and adults behave similarly. Commercially they are reared on bran flakes infested with a flour mite or other stored-product mite such as *Acarus siro*.

Crop/pest associations
A. cucumeris are introduced to the crop with the rearing medium, usually diluted with a carrier material such as vermiculite granules, placed in shaker bottles or tubes. Pure bran flakes infested with the prey mite and predator are used in sachets to provide a continuous release of predators over a 6–8 week period. These sachets are placed on growing plants and over a period of weeks will treat many leaves on the surrounding area. If the product is examined closely the slow moving, hairy, white flour mites can be seen and may be mistaken for the predator. This predator attacks mainly the first instar thrips larva, so it is necessary to maintain an active population of mites on plants to gain maximum levels of pest control. It is quite usual to introduce *A. cucumeris* as a preventive treatment, however, on plants that flower continuously and produce pollen such as sweet pepper; the mite will readily establish from a single introduction.

Influence on growing practices
A. cucumeris is susceptible to most insecticides and several fungicides used in crop protection. Low humidities early in the growing season can disrupt the development of this predatory mite, requiring repeat introductions for several plant types. This is one of the cheapest predators to buy in large numbers and on several ornamental pot plant crops is used as 'living pesticide', being introduced weekly at rates of between 100–300 mites/m².

AMBLYSEIUS (IPHISEIUS) DEGENERANS (BERLESE) (300)

Species characteristics
A shiny black, oval shaped mite 1 mm in length that rapidly runs over leaves, *Amblyseius degenerans* originates in the Mediterranean region and north Africa. It feeds on a wide range of food including thrips larvae, spider mites and other small arthropod prey, which it sucks dry. The mites are able to survive and reproduce on a diet of pollen, but when food is limited they can be strongly cannibalistic with females eating males and all immature stages.

Life cycle
Adult females deposit eggs that are initially transparent but turn a brown colour as they mature on leaf hairs usually at the junction of veins and at curled leaf edges. Unusually, the mites can lay their eggs onto those laid earlier, even when eggs were laid by other females, giving rise to quite large egg clusters being produced at favoured sites. Eggs hatch after a couple of days at 25°C (77°F) and can develop to adulthood within a week at this temperature. Male mites attach themselves to female protonymphs and mating occurs almost immediately the young female emerges.

Crop/pest associations
A. degenerans establishes well on most smooth leafed plants that have a continuous production of pollen, including citrus and sweet pepper plants. Like *A. cucumeris* the mite can be introduced by inoculation to young plants once they have begun to flower and produce pollen, to prevent the establishment of thrips. Trials in Holland have used banker plants of castor *Ricinus communis*, placed close to rows of sweet pepper plants for the production of this predator. The castor leaves are then periodically removed for placement on the crop in areas of pest increase.

Influence on growing practices
A. degenerans is sensitive to many fungicides and insecticides in common horticultural use; indeed the vapourization of sulphur to control powdery mildew causes a reduction in predator numbers. On pepper it has been shown to attack larger thrips (unlike *A. cucumeris* which is restricted to first instar thrips larvae) and to tolerate lower humidity levels. This mite has not been shown to control thrips populations on any crop other than sweet pepper.

299 *Amblyseius cucumeris* adult mite and egg.

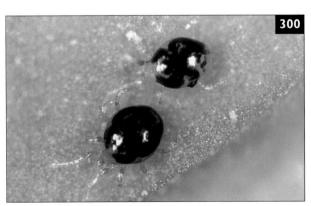

300 *Amblyseius degenerans* adult predatory mites.

AMBLYSEIUS (TYPHLODROMIPS) MONTDORENSIS (SCHICHA) (301)

Species characteristics

Approximately 1 mm in length, the predatory mite *Amblyseius montdorensis* was first described by Schicha in 1979 from mites collected in Fiji, New Caledonia, New Hebrides, Tahiti and Queensland Australia, where it is widely distributed in the sub-tropical areas. This generalist feeder may be found attacking small arthropods such as rust and gall mites (Eriophyidae), tarsonemid mites, spider mites and thrips.

Life cycle

Female mites lay eggs on the leaf surface. These hatch after a day or so to produce a six-legged larva that passes two nymphal stages to reach adulthood in under a week at 25°C (77°F).

Crop/pest associations

Adults and older nymphs show a good ability to disperse through plant canopies and even between plants in search of pollen or prey. This voracious predator has a high reproductive rate and can readily establish on several leaf and plant types. Current rates of introduction are between 5–20 mites/m² on two occasions, compared to *A. cucumeris* that is normally introduced at 100–300 mites/m² weekly, depending on the crop.

Influence on growing practices

This predatory mite is still under evaluation in much of Europe and North America. However, studies have indicated that development of *A. montdorensis* is likely to be severely reduced at temperatures below 17°C (63°F) and humidities below 60%. Even in crops with a high daytime temperature, it may not establish during winter and spring.

HYPOASPIS MILES (BERLESE) HYPOASPIS ACULEIFER (CANESTRINI) (302–304)

Species characteristics

Hypoaspis spp. are small, soil-dwelling mites inhabiting the top few centimetres of compost; they are also recorded from stored products, such as spoiled flour, rodent and occasionally bird nests where they feed on animal parasitoid mites. The mites are predatory, feeding on sciarid larvae and other insects or mites associated with its habitat. Female mites are the largest life stage, being up to 1 mm long, and like males possess a pale brown dorsal shield whereas immatures are white in colour.

Life cycle

The adult female deposits her oval white eggs on the soil surface and amongst the top layers of compost. These hatch into a six-legged larva which pass through two eight-legged nymphal stages to reach adulthood some 18 days later at 20°C (68°F).

Crop/pest associations

Recent research has shown *H. miles* to be very efficient in controlling sciarid fly larvae in a range of composts and growing conditions, including mushroom houses. Other work has indicated a potential for control of thrips larvae, particularly when they pupate on the ground. *H. aculeifer* has better activity against bulb scale mites (*Rhizoglyphus* spp.) making this species preferable for commercial use against these pests. Both species have shown a high tolerance to starvation as they can survive for 6–8 weeks in the absence of food, although water is required. When a mite captures its prey it inserts its saw-like mouth parts which slice the internal tissues; these are then sucked up to leave a shrivelled cadaver.

Influence on growing practices

Hypoaspis spp. are commercially available and are becoming an important adjunct to the biological armoury where soil pests require compatible control measures. Temperatures below 11°C (52°F) cause inactivity and a cessation in egg hatch, whereas activity remains high at up to 30°C (86°F). Pesticides such as diazinon and many other folia applied sprays have little effect on these mites.

301 *Amblyseius montdorensis* adult mites.

302 *Hypoaspis miles* attacking a sciarid fly larva.

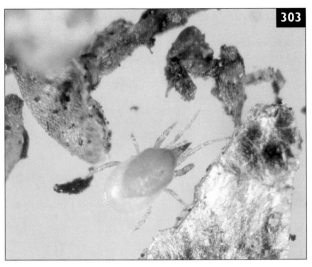

303 *H. miles* adult mite.

304 *H. aculeifer* adult (note the difference in the dorsal shield).

PHYTOSEIULUS PERSIMILIS (ATHIAS-HENRIOT) (305, 306

Species characteristics
The predatory mite *Phytoseiulus persimilis* is the principal biological control agent for the glasshouse spider mite *Tetranychus urticae*, and can be easily differentiated from its host by the pear-shaped body and rapid movement. All but the larval stage are predatory and will eat all stages of spider mite.

Life cycle
Adult females lay up to five eggs per day, depositing them close to the host. Eggs are oval and almost twice the size of spider mite eggs (spider mite eggs are perfectly spherical). On hatching, the six-legged larva moves little and does not feed but soon changes to a protonymph which then starts to feed. Unlike spider mites, *P. persimilis* has no resting stages during its nymphal development. After the deutonymph stage comes the adult, which normally mates within a few hours of development and may mate several times. Unmated females do not produce eggs.

Crop/pest associations
P. persimilis was accidentally introduced to Germany on a shipment of orchids from Chile in 1958; from there it has been introduced to all European countries and is now used throughout most of the world. The predator can be used wherever *T. urticae* is found, although its activity can be hampered on particularly smooth leaved plants such as carnation or on leaves with sticky hairs (trichomes), e.g. tomato. Tomato is a particularly difficult plant for *P. persimilis* activity as the stem is also covered in sticky hairs. Mobility of the mite is improved when leaves touch; on some crops where leaf contact is minimal netting or even string may be used to provide walk-ways.

Influence on growing practices
Temperature is possibly the most important factor for *P. persimilis*, there being little activity below 12°C (54°F), while above 35°C (95°F) the mite ceases feeding and moves down the plant to cooler, shady areas. However, at 20–22°C (68–72°F) the mite's development time from egg to adult is twice as fast as the spider mite. Maximum egg production is between 17 and 28°C (63–82°F) and as the normal male to female ratio is 1:4 it can be seen why this mite is so successful a predator. Humidity is also important: very high humidity (above 90%) is detrimental and below 55% can markedly disrupt egg survival.

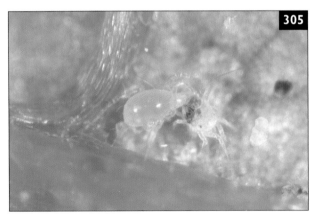

305 *Phytoseiulus persimilis* nymph attacking *Tetranychus urticae*.

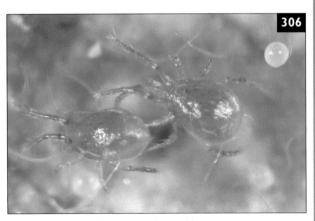

306 *P. persimilis* adults on *T. urticae* webbing.

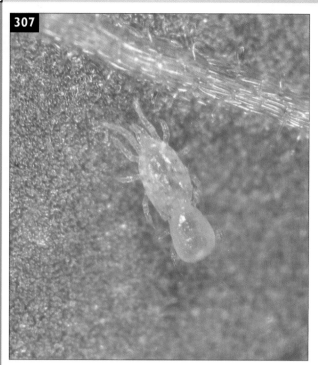

307 *Typhlodromus pyri* mating pair.

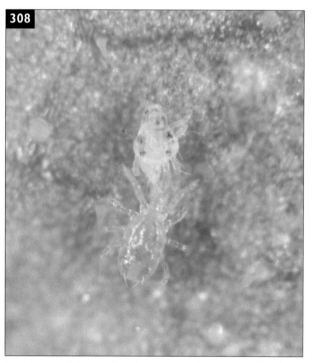

308 *T. pyri* adult attacking *Tetranychus urticae* (2-spotted spider mite).

TYPHLODROMUS PYRI (SCHEUTEN) (307, 308)

Species characteristics
Typhlodromus pyri is a small fast moving predatory mite found on a wide range of trees, often on the underside of leaves close to the mid vein. Adult females are pale with a narrow parallel sided body, approximately 0.3 mm in length. Eggs are translucent and are oval shaped, approximately 0.16 mm × 0.11 mm. Larvae hatch but do not feed before developing into protonymphs which resemble the adults in shape.

Life cycle
Females over-winter in crevices in the bark and emerge in the spring when they are found at high densities on the early leaves of vines and fruit trees. Eggs are usually laid singly, on the underside of leaves often close to the mid vein. Development to adult stage takes about two weeks at 22°C (72°F). There are four or more generations per year depending on climatic conditions.

Crop/pest associations
T. pyri is an important predator of spider mites and rust mites in apple and pear orchards, as well as in vineyards in temperate climates. In warmer regions different phytoseiid species such as *Amblyseius abberans* and *Amblysieus* (*Neioseiulus*) *californicus* appear to occupy a similar niche. When there is no prey present *T. pyri* can also feed on pollen, reaching very high population levels by this means. Mites are rarely found on leaves exposed to bright sunlight and during the season tend to concentrate within the mid canopy.

Influence on growing practices
With careful use of only selective fungicides and insecticides predatory mites can provide season-long control of spider mites and prevent any need for acaricide use. Like most predatory Phytoseiidae, *T. pyri* is very sensitive to pyrethroid insecticides and if predatory mites are to be encouraged use of such insecticides should be avoided. Some populations of *T. pyri*, particularly in southern Germany, have developed resistance to a wide range of pesticides, particularly organophosphates and dithiocarbamates. Naturally occurring populations can be augmented by the release of commercially-reared mites.

Chilopoda

CENTIPEDES

LITHOBIUS FORFICATUS (LINNAEUS)
HAPLOPHILUS SUBTERRANEUS (SHAW)
(309, 310)

Species characteristics

Centipedes, or hundred-legged worms, are not insects. They have a flattened, elongated body, with many segments, each bearing two legs (except the first behind the head and the last two). They are predatory against a wide range of soil inhabiting organisms. Two will be described in this piece: *Lithobius forficatus* and a *Haplophilus* species; both are known as garden centipedes where, once disturbed they can be found scurrying around in moist areas. All centipedes have a distinct head that carries a pair of long, slender antennae made up of many joints and may reach over one-third of the body length, as in *L. forficatus*. The first segment behind the head bears a pair of sharp claws containing poison glands that are used to seize and kill the prey. In some species the 'bite' is harmful to humans but rarely lethal; even the common *L. forficatus*, at 3 cm in length can inflict a painful 'bite' if handled roughly. Centipedes of the Geophilidae family are longer (up to 12 cm) and worm like with a more rounded body, short antennae and no eyes. They also possess glands used to spin a secretion that binds eggs and spermatozoa together. Some species of *Geophilus* have over 150 legs.

Millipedes, or thousand-legged worms, are also not insects. They have a more rounded body with four legs on each segment, do not possess poison glands and generally have short antennae. They are plant feeders and scavengers of other food sources. An irritating, odorous substance may be secreted as a defence against attack that may linger on hands and clothing.

Life cycle

Centipedes are relatively long lived, with some species known to live for up to six years. They over-winter as adults in dark humid areas such as compost heaps, leaf litter, under rotting timber and other protected places. Egg laying begins in the spring and continues through much of the summer months. Female centipedes often remain with their eggs to prevent them becoming desiccated or from fungal attack if too moist. They may be seen licking the eggs, a process thought to involve the secretion of a fungicidal substance. Eggs usually hatch after a week or so to an eight-legged immature centipede and, having no larval stage, grow by adding more segments posteriorly, each with a pair of legs. Young centipedes may be confused with beetle larvae, particularly those of rove and carabid beetles. However, a quick leg count will easily identify one from the other: insect larvae either possess three pairs of legs or none at all.

Crop/pest associations

These predators are active hunters of many soil dwelling organisms including earthworms, millipedes, young slugs and snails, spiders, symphilids, woodlice, insect eggs and beetle grubs. *H. subterraneus* may also feed on plant roots but generally do not cause economic damage. Their generally low numbers are attributed to their longevity and ability to search for prey over a large area; they can also be cannibalistic and in their juvenile stage fall victim to other predators as well as to older centipedes.

Influence on growing practices

Although common in most gardens, their need for a moist dark environment restricts centipedes from intensive agriculture and places where the soil regularly dries to a depth of more than a few centimetres.

309 *Lithobius forficatus* (Linnaeus) (centipede) under a log (photograph courtesy of Peter Wilson/Holt Studios).

310 *Haplophilus subterraneus*.

SECTION 4:
ENTOMOPATHOGENS

- NEMATODES
- BACTERIA
- FUNGI
- BACULOVIRUSES

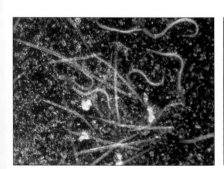

Diseases of insects and mites play an important role as natural enemies of many major pest species throughout the world. They may infect and kill a few individual hosts, but under favourable conditions may infect whole colonies killing many millions of organisms, spreading as an epizootic infection. These conditions generally include a high pest density where the infection can spread easily between individuals, and for fungi and nematodes a warm, moist environment is essential. Commercialization of several entomopathogens has taken effect throughout the world, but due to registration requirements (they are often regarded as pesticides) their use as bio-insecticides may be restricted in some countries. Representative entomopathogens are presented here and include nematodes, bacteria, fungi, and viruses (**311–314**).

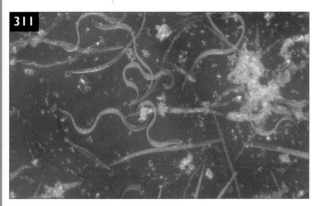

311 *Heterorhabditis* sp. free-living nematodes.

313 *Pieris brassicae* (large white butterfly) caterpillar killed by *Bacillus thuringiensis*.

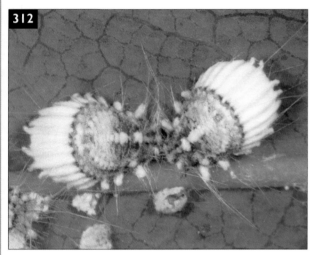

312 *Icerya purchasi* (cottony cushion scale) infected with the fungal pathogen *Beauveria bassiana*.

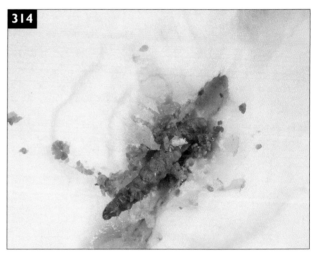

314 *Cydia pomonella* (Linnaeus) (codling moth) caterpillar killed by *C. pomonella* granulovirus (CpGV – Mexican).

Nematodes

ROUNDWORMS

Commonly known as roundworms, these often-minute organisms are relatively simple, being bilaterally symmetrical, elongated and tapered at both ends. The species profiled here are facultative parasitoids that, although found in nature, are all capable of being mass-produced on artificial diets by fermentation processes and are commercially used as biological control agents. Unlike plant parasitoid nematodes, these entomopathogenic species have symbiotic bacteria in their alimentary tract that are the killing agent in a nematode attack. Once the nematode is inside the host and feeding on the hemolymph it defecates a small pellet of bacteria which, under the right temperature conditions, quickly kill the host after only 2–3 days. The nematodes then reproduce in the soup of bacteria and hemolymph leaving the cadaver as third stage infective larvae. These are unusually resistant to adverse environmental conditions and can survive several months as 'dauer larvae'.

HETERORHABDITIS MEGIDIS (POINAR, JACKSON, AND KLEIN) STEINERNEMA FELTIAE (FILIPJEV) STEINERNEMA KRAUSSEI (STEINER) (315–318)

Species characteristics

Entomopathogenic nematodes are minute, non-segmented organisms that are free-living in peat and soil compost, and proactively seek out their prey. They are a milky white in colour and almost impossible to see when in soil; however, when extracted in water they may be seen with basic magnification as individual 'S'-shaped worms.

Life cycle

Once a host insect larva is found, infective nematodes enter the body through natural openings (*Heterorhabditis* spp. can also penetrate the insect cuticle). Entomopathogenic nematodes carry symbiotic insect-pathogenic bacteria within their gut. *Heterorhabditis* spp. are associated with *Photorhabdus* spp. of bacteria that in the latter stages of infection give a reddish colour to the host larva, whereas in *Steinernema* spp. of nematodes there are *Xenorhabdus* spp. of bacteria. Soon after host penetration the bacteria are released and under suitable temperature conditions multiply, spreading rapidly throughout the insect causing septicaemia and death, usually within 48 hours. The nematode feeds on the bacteria and digested host tissue, reproducing to form thousands of infective larval nematodes that are released from the cadaver some 10–14 days later.

Crop/pest associations

Entomopathogenic nematodes are mainly used for control of vine weevil larvae (*Heterorhabditis* spp.) and sciarid fly larvae (*Steinernema* spp.), although other soil dwelling insects can also be attacked. Recent research has led to the use of a specially formulated steinernematid nematode product sprayed on to leaves, to kill leaf miners, scale insects and thrips. However, desiccation is a particular problem and care is required for successful pest control. Entomopathogenic nematodes are usually applied as a soil drench and can be used as both preventative and curative treatments. Other uses for nematodes include control of turf pests such as chafer grubs and leatherjackets, with a drench application in the late summer/early autumn ensuring best targeting of the most susceptible stages.

Influence on growing practices

Most entomopathogenic nematodes are inactive at temperatures below 12°C (54°F). This limits their area of activity mainly to protected crops where the compost can be maintained at a suitable temperature. They can be used successfully outdoors from late spring to early autumn for control of pests in container grown plants. However, a new strain of the nematode *Steinernema kraussei*, has been sold which is active down to 5°C (40°F) against black vine weevil (*Otiorhynchus sulcatus*) and enables the use of nematodes from early spring to late autumn. The worms are highly susceptible to desiccation particularly when used in containers kept in glasshouses or conservatories. Most pesticides are safe to use with nematodes except some soil-applied drenches and those with nematacidal activity.

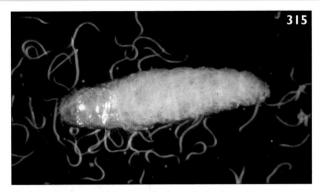

315 Sciarid pupa with nematodes from the body cavity.

316 Dead *Otiorhychus sulcatus* (vine weevil) larva with nematodes (*Steinernema carpocapsae*) released from the body cavity.

317 Red coloration of a dead *O. sulcatus* larva parasitized by *Heterorhabditis* sp.

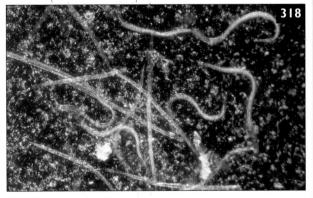

318 *Steinernema* sp. free-living nematodes.

PHASMARHABDITIS HERMAPHRODITA (SCHNEIDER) (319–324)

Species characteristics

Phasmarhabditis hermaphrodita is a parasitoid nematode first isolated from field slugs showing signs of nematode infection in southern UK. Infective slug nematodes are microscopic at 1097 μm × 27 μm (1000 μm = 1 mm). Their natural habitat is soil where they can survive as the infective juvenile stage for long periods under the right conditions but only in small numbers. At this stage the nematodes have no mouth or anus and so do not feed, but survive using the fat stored in their bodies. Parasitoid nematodes have associated bacteria in their bodies which, in combination with the nematode, is invariably the cause of the host organism's death. Commercially grown *P. hermaphrodita* are associated with the bacteria *Moraxella osloensis*.

Life cycle

Reproduction can only occur on suitable invertebrate host organism tissue. *P. hermaphrodita* move short distances in the soil or compost to seek out new hosts providing the medium is moist and not too compacted. When a slug is encountered the nematodes enter the body through a pore at the rear of the mantle called the pneumostome. They start to develop from infective juveniles to adults; this triggers the release of the bacteria, which begin to multiply spreading the infection to the rest of the slug's body. The presence of the bacteria and increasing numbers of nematodes can be seen as a swelling of the mantle that results in the slug's death a few days after infection.

Crop/pest associations

P. hermaphrodita is most pathogenic against the grey field slug *Deroceras reticulatum* and *Arion* species but can also kill other slugs and some snails. Slug feeding is inhibited a few days after infection and subsequent plant damage is rapidly reduced. Dead slugs tend to remain hidden below ground where they disintegrate after releasing the next generation of infective juveniles. This recycling of nematodes does not significantly increase or extend pest control for long periods.

Influence on growing practices

Nematodes are most effective when the soil temperature is between 5 and 20°C (40 and 68°F); applications can be made at any time of year providing the above conditions can be achieved (freezing will kill them). Natural populations of parasitoid nematodes are usually present in relatively low numbers and do not kill many organisms. However, an application of these nematodes results in a temporary increase, which can provide good control. As the parasitoids do not persist in large numbers for long periods of time they are unlikely to cause a significant disruption to the ecosystem. Although found in the UK and sold in parts of Europe this nematode or similar species have not, as yet, been isolated in North America.

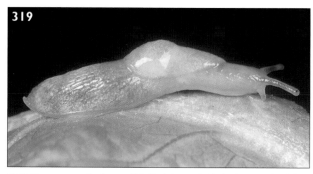

319 *Deroceras reticulatum* (Muller) (grey field slug) parasitized by *Phasmarhabditis hermaphrodita* showing its swollen mantle.

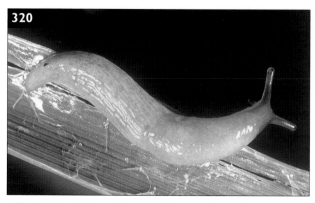

320 Uninfected *D. reticulatum* with a normal mantle.

321 *D. reticulatum* parasitized by *P. hermaphrodita*.

322 *P. hermaphrodita* nematodes developing in a dead *D. reticulatum*.

323 Snail parasitized by *P. hermaphrodita*.

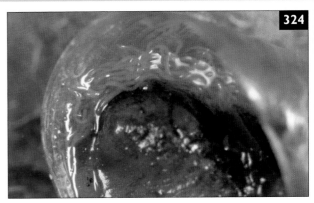

324 Snail parasitized by *P. hermaphrodita* showing the developing nematodes.

Bacteria

BACILLUS THURINGIENSIS (BERLINER) (325, 326)

Species characteristics

Bacteria are simple unicellular organisms, lacking a cell nucleus and mitochondria; reproduction is by binary division, either within an insect host or commercially by fermentation process using artificial mediums. *Bacillus thuringiensis* (*Bt*) is a spore forming bacteria that was first isolated in Japan in 1902 from infected silkworms. In its vegetative state, this gram-positive, aerobic bacterium measures 3–5 µm × 1.0–1.2 µm (1000 µm = 1 mm). There are several strains that have different spectra of activity against insects, caterpillars, mosquito larvae and certain beetle larvae including their adults. This range of activity is determined by the matrix of complex protein toxin crystals within the bacterial spore. Bi-pyramidal crystals (like two Egyptian pyramids fixed base to base) range in size and contain up to five different toxic protein sub-units. However, as no single strain has activity against all the target pests, it is now possible to combine two strains together and widen the range of activity. This process is known as transconjugation and has led to some patented bio-insecticide products. Through genetic manipulation it is also possible to transfer the toxic protein genes into plants, thus protecting them from caterpillar attack.

Life cycle

The active ingredients of formulated *Bt* are viable spores and toxic protein crystals. Activity within a larval insect is dependent on ingestion of the crystals. Once ingested, pH conditions (pH >9) and gut enzymes of the insect rapidly break the crystals down to toxic sub-units which attack the mid gut. Paralysis of the gut occurs within a few hours. Feeding and movement cease soon after, and cells of the gut become extensively damaged leading to insect death after a day or so. Dead insects fall to the ground or stick to leaves and slowly disintegrate.

Crop/pest associations

Unprotected, leaf-feeding caterpillars are the easiest target to control and also make up the largest commercial usage of *Bt* worldwide. Insects sheltering within folded or rolled leaves, plant stems or those that live in silken webs are more difficult to target, and insects that have burrowed into leaf or stem are impossible to control with sprays of *Bt*. Due to the specific requirements of the crystal which only occur within the gut of certain insects, *Bt* is much safer to non-target organisms (including man) than many pesticides.

Influence on growing practices

Bt is usually applied as high volume sprays to thoroughly wet the foliage. However, treatments by thermal fogging machines and other low volume apparatus have given excellent results. The toxic crystals may be denatured by ultra violet (UV) radiation, as may occur in open field crops, orchards and forestry after a few days of sunshine. Under glass the activity usually remains for up to a week after application.

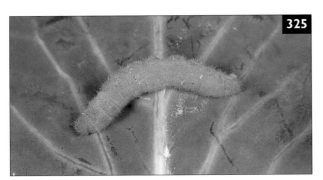

325 *Pieris rapae* (Linnaeus) (small white butterfly) caterpillar recently killed by *Bacillus thuringiensis*.

326 *P. rapae* caterpillar several days after treatment with *B. thuringiensis*.

Fungi

Fungal infections of insects are one of the most common forms of disease-causing pathogen found in nature, particularly in warm humid environments, or following a period of such weather conditions. Fungal spores landing on an insect can germinate producing a germ tube that actively penetrates the cuticle and colonize the host tissues with hyphae. These can grow throughout the body leading to host death after a few days. If conditions are favourable reproductive spores will be formed either internally or externally as conidia, resistant spores or sporangia. Many hundred thousand spores may be produced from each infected host which, under the right conditions, can spread to other insects as an epizootic infection. Several fungal pathogens are commercially produced as bio-insecticides and, although naturally occurring throughout the world, often require registration similar to chemical pesticides that may hinder their availability.

BEAUVERIA BASSIANA (BALSAMO AND VUILLEMIN) (327–329)

Species characteristics
There are several naturally occurring species and strains of insect pathogenic fungus within the *Beauveria* genus. *B. bassiana* is in commercial production and likely to be a registered product in several countries throughout the world over the next few years. This fungus is used as a contact mycoinsecticide but survives a relatively short period of time when exposed on a leaf surface. Most commercial formulations are based on infective spores (conidia) recovered from solid substrate production systems, that may be packaged as an emulsifiable suspension in oil or as a dry water dispersible powder.

Life cycle
The conidium is non-motile and asexual. Once contact has been made with the target organism, the conidia adhere to the cuticle where they germinate to produce a germ tube that penetrates the host's body. This invasive infection can kill the insect in 3–7 days, leaving a white mass of spores which can spread to other insects.

Crop/pest associations
B. bassiana has a very wide host range and is reported to control aphids, thrips, whitefly, sciarid fly, scatella fly, mealybug and vine weevil larvae effectively. It will also infect scale insects, spider mites and leaf-feeding caterpillars under ideal conditions. These entomopathogenic fungi have low mammalian toxicity and can infect a high proportion of pest organisms, often resulting in fungal epizootics.

327 *Planococcus* sp. (mealybugs) killed by *Beauveria bassiana*.

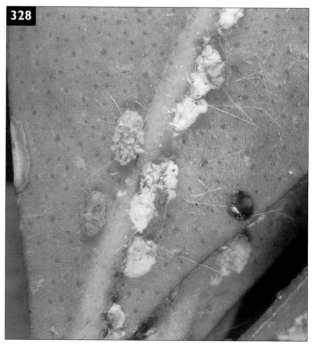

328 *Planococcus* sp. killed by *B. bassiana*.

Influence on growing practices

B. bassiana can be formulated to infect insects over a range of conditions. Infected insects may cause a cosmetic problem on certain crops due to the presence of dead bodies, as may occur when high numbers of pests are present before the fungus is established. Fungicides used to control plant pathogens may disrupt these myco-insecticides; however, several insecticides and in particular chitin inhibiting insect growth regulators are compatible and used safely within an ICM programme.

CONIDIOBOLUS SPP. (330, 331)

Species characteristics

There may be several species of *Conidiobolus* in the order Entomophthoraceae that infect sciarid fly and other soil associated organisms. Infection of the larva causes it to change its normal behaviour (which is to avoid light by living in the soil where they feed on plant roots) and move to the soil surface to die. Dead, infected larvae may be found on the soil surface as milky-white threads 8–10 mm in length and up to 2 mm in diameter. There are no commercial products containing these fungi at present but methods of encouraging their activity are planned.

Life cycle

Conidiophores on the surface of an infected sciarid larva rupture to produce showers of sticky conidia. These spores infect other larvae by contact via movement through or across the soil; adult flies are also likely to transmit the infection. Conidia contact the host larva, produce hyphae that penetrate the cuticle and invade body tissues. As the host is overcome with fungal growth it changes to a grey/brown colour and moves upwards finally to rest in the open, where it turns milky-white during sporulation when the conidiophores forcibly discharge further conidia.

Crop/pest associations

Infections recorded so far in the UK have all been associated with peat-based growing media, but it is likely that similar media such as coir and bark would be suitable for infection. This group of soil-active entomophthoralean fungi are mainly found on sciarid larvae (*Bradysia* spp.), but it is possible that other organisms inhabiting similar environments such as shore flies (*Scatella [stagnalis] tenuicosta*) could become infected. *Conidiobolus* spp. are also associated with several aphid species and may be found through the temperate regions particularly on cereal crops.

Influence on growing practices

Fungicides applied to control root diseases such as *Pythium*, *Phytopthora* and *Thieliviopsis*, which are easily spread by sciarid flies, may seriously disrupt these naturally occurring entomopathogens. Resting stages have been found for some *Conidiobolus* spp. and are likely to be produced when adverse conditions prevail, enabling them to survive between cropping cycles. In suitable conditions a high level of infection is possible resulting in fungal epizootics that may persist between crops. The presence of dead bodies on the soil surface may cause cosmetic problems but they tend to disintegrate after a few days leaving little sign of insect or fungal presence.

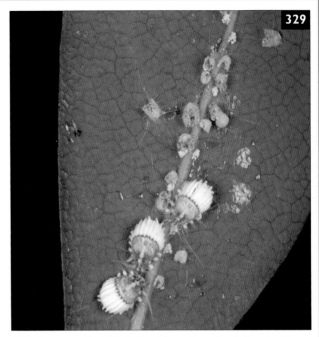

329 *Icerya purchasi* (Maskell) adults and crawlers infected with *B. bassiana*.

330 Sciarid fly larvae on a pot plant's soil surface killed by a naturally occurring entomophthoralean fungus *Conidiobolus* spp.

331 Close up of sciarid larva killed by an entomophthoralean fungus *Conidiobolus* spp.

PANDORA (=ERYNIA) NEOAPHIDIS (REMAUDIERE, HENNEBERT AND HUMBER) (332)

Species characteristics
Erynia neoaphidis is one of a group of entomopathogenic (insect attacking) fungi from the order Entomophthoraceae, found throughout the world where they readily form epizootic infections; indeed in some years entomopathogenic fungi kill more insects than any of the arthropod parasitoids and predators.

Life cycle
Conidia contact the host and under humid conditions rapidly penetrate the cuticle with hyphae that invade the body tissues. Death occurs a day or so after initial infection, but outward signs of infection may take several days to appear. The cadaver is attached to the plant by thin stalk-like rhizoids that terminate in a flattened disc structure. Ripe conidiophores rupture and forcibly discharge their conidia into the air to spread further infection.

Crop/pest associations
Dead aphids take on a pale brown to orange-red colour as they become covered in fine velvety spores. Other species of entomophthoralean fungi may be found infecting Diptera, Homoptera, Lepidoptera and Orthoptera.

Although they are regarded as beneficial to most growers, high numbers on edible leafy salad crops may cause cosmetic damage and a reduction in marketability. To date there are no commercial preparations based on *Erynia* spp.

Influence on growing practices
These insect pathogenic fungi are highly virulent and can provide high levels of pest control. They are more common where aphids are more abundant and usually make their appearance a few weeks after the initial aphid infestation. Crops receiving overhead irrigation can frequently double the incidence and spread of entomopathogenic fungi. The use of fungicides to control plant pathogens can adversely affect most of these insect pathogens.

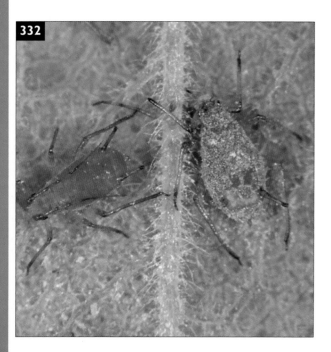

VERTICILLIUM LECANII (ZIMMERMAN AND VIEGAS) (333–338)

Species characteristics
The insect pathogenic fungus *Verticillium lecanii* contains several strains which differ in their host range and may be very host specific. Its fluffy white halo-like appearance can be found around infected insects. It is common throughout the tropics where it may be found infecting aphids, mites, scale insects and whitefly; it is also a saprophyte and hyperparasitoid of leaf spots, powdery mildews and rusts. However, it cannot parasitize plants, birds, fish or mammals.

Life cycle
Starting with either spores from a commercial product or from an infected insect, contact must be made directly with the host cuticle. Fresh spores are sticky and so will adhere to a passing insect. Germination and subsequent penetration of the host cuticle requires high humidity (above 95%) for about 12 hours; once the fungus has begun growing in the insect the humidity requirement is greatly reduced. Infected aphids continue feeding and can even produce healthy live young until quite late in the infection process. After 5–10 days, depending on temperature and humidity, the insect dies and is covered by a fluffy white mass of spores. For the infection process to continue high humidity is again required.

Crop/pest associations
Commercially there are two strains of *V. lecanii* available, one is more specific for aphids and the other can infect both thrips and whitefly. If all these pest are present on the crop both strains can be mixed to provide a wider spectrum of activity. They can also be mixed with *Bacillus thuringiensis* for caterpillar control.

Influence on growing practices
Temperature is not critical between about 15–28°C (59–82°F). Temperatures above (up to 38°C [100°F]) and below this range (down to 2°C [36°F]) will not kill the fungus but arrest its development until suitable conditions return. Humidity however, is the most important factor influencing the germination, infection and spread of *V. lecanii* in a pest population. In cucumber crops the conditions can be achieved most nights, but on tomato and most other crops the humidity requirement is only realized during spring and autumn. Research has shown that fogging water above the crop for 40 hours per week will provide the necessary conditions without causing undue problems to the plants.

332 *Macrosiphum rosae* (Linnaeus) (rose aphids) on the right killed by the entomophthoralean fungus *Pandora neoaphidis.*

333 An alate aphid killed by *Verticillium lecanii*.

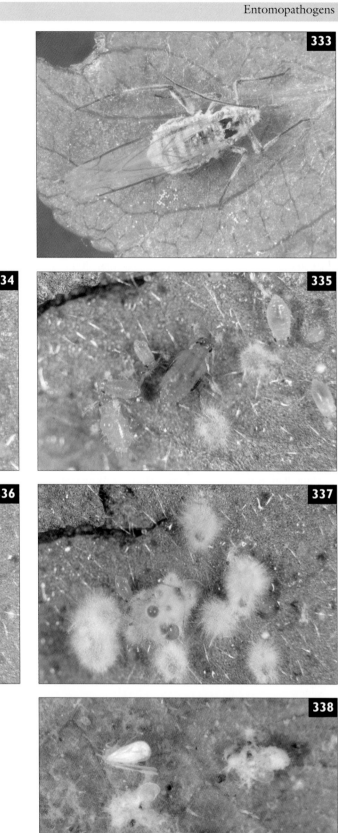

334–337 Four stages in the development of *V. lecanii* on an aphid colony.

338 *Trialeurodes vaporariorum* (glasshouse whitefly) killed by *V. lecanii*.

Baculoviruses

BACULOVIRUSES (339, 340)

Species characteristics

Baculoviruses belong to a family of double-stranded DNA viruses in which the virions are embedded in a crystalline proteinaceous occlusion body. They are mostly associated with lepidopteran larvae although some viruses attack other insects including caddisfly, cranefly, mosquitoes and sawflies. Historically, this group of viruses has been recorded for over 2000 years, initially from infected silkworm caterpillars (*Bombix mori*). They are also most likely to account for the epizootics that have frequently decimated caterpillar populations in various parts of the world. There are two major types of baculoviruses: nucleopolyhedroviruses (NPVs) and granuloviruses (GVs). Within the NPVs are rod-shaped particles (virions) protected in a membranous envelope containing either single or groups of virions which are embedded in a proteinaceous, polyhedral-shaped occlusion body. They range in size from 1–5 nm in diameter and form in the nuclei of infected cells. GVs are structurally similar to NPVs but the virions are occluded individually in small bodies referred to as granules that have an average size of approximately 150 nm × 400–600 nm.

Life cycle

All viruses must reproduce in the cells of living organisms by invading individual cells to replicate, firstly in the nucleus and after rupturing the nuclear membrane, in the cytoplasm. The predominant route of viral infection is by ingestion of inoculated plant material. Once in the alkaline juices of the caterpillar mid gut the protective granules and polyhedra surrounding the virions are rapidly digested. The released virions pass through the peritrophic membrane to infect various body cells. As a NPV infection progresses, the body may become swollen and takes on a glossy appearance; with a reasonable light microscope it may be possible to see white polyhedra within swollen cells. The final stages of infection are seen as a liquefaction of the caterpillar body, which typically hang head down by their prolegs or in an inverted 'V'. The cuticle then ruptures after a few hours releasing many millions of polyhedra. There are two types of GVs, referred to as fast and slow. Caterpillars infected with slow GVs always kill the host in its final larval instar, regardless of when it became infected, and are observable as creamy white to yellow patches of fat cells packed with viral granules. Fast GVs kill at the same rate as NPVs.

Crop/pest associations

Entomopathogenic viruses often have a very narrow insect host range, usually restricted to just one or two species and none are known to have any vertebrate associations. The occlusion bodies offer great protection for the virus; many moth species have only one or two generations each year so the virus must be able to replicate rapidly enough to complete its cycle and then be able to survive until the following year. Some viruses are known to have survived for several decades in the soil before entering a suitable host insect and still be infectious.

339 *Pieris rapae* (small white butterfly) caterpillar with lighter colouration is beginning to show the effects of *P. rapae* granulovirus (PrGV).

340 Dead *P. rapae* caterpillar after treatment with *P. rapae* granulovirus (PrGV).

Influence on growing practices

Baculoviruses are generally regarded as specific insect pathogens that show a high level of environmental safety and pest selectivity. They show great potential as bio-insecticides that can be targeted to a particular pest; for example, in Brazil over 1 million hectares of soybeans are treated annually to control the velvet-bean caterpillar (*Anticarsia gemmatalis*). In several European countries virus preparations are commercially available to control apple codling moth larvae. It is likely that many baculoviruses will be registered for commercial use as bio-insecticides throughout the world.

References

Aldridge, C. and Carter, N. (1992) The principles of risk assessment for non-target arthropods: a UK registration perspective. Interpretation of pesticide effects on beneficial arthropods. *Aspects of Applied Biology* **31**: 149–156.

Baur, R., Remund, U., Kauer, S. and Boller, E. (1998) Seasonal and spatial dynamics of *Empoasca vitis* and its egg parasitoids in vineyards in Northern Switzerland. Proceedings of the IOBC/WPRS working group Viticulture, March 4–7, 1997, Godollo, Hungary. *IOBC/WPRS Bulletin* **21**(2):71–72.

Boller, E.F. (2001) Functional biodiversity and agro-ecosystems management: 1. Identified information gaps. Integrated Fruit Production. *IOBC/WPRS Bulletin* **24**(5):1–4.

Brown, M.W. (2001) Functional biodiversity and agro-ecosystems management: 2. Role in integrated fruit production. *IOBC/WPRS Bulletin* **24**(5):5–11.

Brown, R.A. (1989) Pesticides and non-target terrestrial invertebrates: an industrial approach. In *Pesticides and Non-target Organisms*, Ed. P.C. Jepson. Intercept: Wimbourne, pp. 19–42.

Cilgi, T. and Vickerman, P. (1994) Selecting arthropod 'indicator species' for environmental impact assessment of pesticides in field studies. *Aspects of Applied Biology* **37**: 131–140.

Cross, J.V., Innocenzi, P. and Hall, D.R. (2000) Integrated Production of Soft Fruits. I*OBC/WPRS Bulletin* **23**(11):67–72.

Cross, J.V. (ed.) (2002) Guidelines for integrated production of pome fruits in Europe. Technical Guideline III, *IOBC/WPRS Bulletin* **25**(8).

Elliott, M., Farnham, A.W., Janes, N.F., Needham, P.H., Pulman, D.A. and Stevenson, J.H. (1973) NRDC 143, a more stable pyrethroid. *Proceeding of the 7th British Insecticide and Fungicide Conference 1973* **2**:721–728.

Everts, J.W., Aukema, B., Hengeveld, R. and Koeman, J.H. (1989) Side-effects of pesticides on ground-dwelling predatory arthropods in arable ecosystems. *Environmental Pollution* **59**: 203–225.

Forsythe, T.G. (1987). Common ground beetles. *Naturalists' Handbook 8*, Richmond Publishing.

Greig-Smith, P. (1991) The Boxworth experience: effects of pesticides on the fauna and flora of cereal fields. In *The Ecology of Temperate Cereal Fields*, Eds. L.G. Firbank, N. Carter, J.F. Darbyshire and G.R. Potts. Blackwell Scientific, London.

Hassan, S.A., Bigler, F., Bogenschutz, H. *et al.* (1983) Results of the second joint testing programme by the IOBC/WPRS working group: pesticides and beneficial arthropods. *Zeitschrift fur Angewandte Entomologie* **95**(2):151–158.

Hassan, S.A., Albert, R., Bigler, F. *et al.* (1987) Results of the third joint testing programme by the IOBC/WPRS working group: pesticides and beneficial organisms. *Journal of Applied Entomology* **103**:92–107.

Hussey, N.W., Read, W.H. and Hesling, J.J. (1969) Pest control: materials and methods. In *The Pests of Protected Cultivation*. Edward Arnold (Publishers) Ltd., London, pp. 9–43.

Hussey, N.W. (1985) History of biological control in protected culture. In *Biological Pest Control*. The glasshouse experience. Ed. N.W. Hussey and N. Scopes. Blandford Press, Poole, pp. 11–22.

Jordan, V.W.L. (1998) The development of integrated arable production systems to meet potential economic and environmental requirements. *Outlook on Agriculture* **27**(3): 145–151.

Luczak, J. (1975) Spider communities of crop fields. *Polish Ecological Studies* **1**:93–110.

Luff, M.L. (1987) Biology of polyphagous ground beetles in agriculture. *Agricultural Zoology Reviews* **2**: 237–278.

MacGill, E.I. (1934) On the biology of *Anagrus atomus*, an egg parasitoid of the leaf-hopper *Erythroneura pallidifrons*. *Parasitology* **26**: 57–63.

Nyffeler, M. and Benz, G. (1987) Spiders in natural pest control: a review. *Journal of Applied Entomology* **103**:321–339.

Nyffeler, M., Sterling, W.L. and Dean, D.A. (1994) Insectivorous activities of spiders in United States field crops. *Journal of Applied Entomology* **118**:113–128.

Paoletti, M.G. and Bressan, M. (1996) Soil invertebrates as bioindicators of human disturbance. *Critical Reviews in Plant Sciences* **15**:21–62.

Péter, G., Kádár, F., Kiss, J. and Tóth, F. (2001) Role of field margin in the winter phenopause of carabid beetles (Coleoptera: Carabidae) in winter wheat fields. Integrated control in cereal crops. *IOBC/WPRS Bulletin* **24**(6):91–94.

Piggott, S.J., Clayton, J., Gwynn, R., Matthews, G.A., Sampson, C. and Wright, D.J. (2000) Improving folia application technologies for ennomopathogenic nematodes. Workshop proceedings; University of Ireland, Maynooth, 13–15th April 2000, pp. 119–127.

Samu, F., Tóth, F., Szinetár, C., Vörös, G. and Botos, E. (2001) Results of a nation-wide survey of spider assemblanges in Hungarian cereal fields: integrated control in cereal crops. *IOBC/WPRS Bulletin* **24**(6):119–127.

Sunderland, K.D., Fraser, A.M. and Dixon, A.F.G. (1986) Distribution of linyphiid spiders in relation to capture of prey in cereal fields. *Pedobiologica* **29**: 367–375.

Sunderland, K.D., Chambers, R.J., Helyer, N.L. and Sopp, P.I. (1992) Integrated pest management of greenhouse crops in Northern Europe. *Horticulture Reviews* **13**:1–47.

Thomas, M.R., Garthwaite, D.G. and Banham, A.R. (1996) *Pesticide Usage Survey Report 141: Arable Farm Crops in Great Britain*. MAFF & SOA.

Toft, S. (1989) Aspects of ground-living spider fauna of two barley fields in Denmark: species richness and phenological synchronisation. *Entomologiske Meddelelser-entomologisk forening Kobenavn* **57**:157–168.

Topping, C.J. and Sunderland, K.D. (1992) Limitation to the use of pitfall traps in ecological studies exemplified by a study of spiders in a field of winter wheat. *Journal of Applied Ecology* **29**: 485–491.

Van Gestel, C.A.M. and van Brummelen, T.C. (1996) Incorporation of the biomarker concept in ecotoxicology calls for a redefinition of terms. *Ecotoxicology* **5**:217–225.

Vickerman, G.P. (1992) The effects of different pesticide regimes on the invertebrate fauna of winter wheat. In *Pesticides and the environment: the Boxworth study*. Eds. P. Grieg-Smith, G.A. Frampton and A. Hardy. HMSO, London.

Further Reading

Alford, D.V. (1991) *A Colour Atlas of Pests of Ornamental Trees, Shrubs and Flowers*. Manson Publishing, London.

Bellows, T.S. and Fisher, T.W. (1999) *Handbook of Biological Control*. Academic Press, San Deigo.

Dreistadt, S.H. (1994) *Pests of Landscape Trees and Shrubs: an Integrated Pest Management Guide*. State-wide IPM Project, University of California, Division of Agriculture and Natural Resources. Publication 3359, Oakland, California.

Ellis, P.R., Entwistle, A.R. and Walkey, D.G.A. (1993) *Pests and Diseases of Alpine Plants*. Alpine Garden Society, Pershore.

Flint, M.L. (1990) *Pests of the Garden and Small Farm: a Growers' Guide to Using Less Pesticide*. State-wide IPM Project, University of California, Division of Agriculture and Natural Resources. Publication 3332, Oakland, California.

Gill, S., Clement, D.L. and Dutky, E. (1999) *Pests and Diseases of Herbaceous Perennials: the Biological Approach*. Ball Publishing, Batavia.

Hoffman, M.P. and Frodsham, A.C. (1993) *Natural Enemies of Vegetable Insect Pests*. Cornell University, Ithaca.

Hoy, M.A., Cunningham, G.L. and Knutson, L. (eds.) (1987) *Biological Control of Pests by Mites*. University of California, Berkeley.

Hussey, N.W. and Scopes, N.E.A. (1985) *Biological Pest Control: The Glasshouse Experience*. Blandford Press, Poole.

Mahr, D.L. and Ridgeway, N.M. (1993) *Biological Control of Insects and Mites, an Introduction to Beneficial Natural Enemies and their Use in Pest Management*. University of Wisconsin, Madison.

Malais, M. and Ravensberg, W. (1992) *Knowing and Recognising : The Biology of Glasshouse Pests and their Natural Enemies*. Koppert, B.V., Berkel en Rodenrijs.

Nechols, J.R., Andres, L.A., Beardsley, J.W., Goeden, R-D. and Jackson, C.G. (1995) Biological control in the western United States: accomplishments and benefits of regional project W-84, 1964–1989. University of California, Division of Agriculture and Natural Resources. Publication 3361, Oakland, California.

Olkowski, W., Daar, S. and Olkowski, H. (1991) *Common Sense Pest Control: Least Toxic Solutions for your Home, Garden, Pets and Community*. Taunton Press, Newtown.

Powell, C.C. and Lindquist, R.K. (1997) *Ball Pest and Disease Manual: Disease, Insect and Mite Control on Flower and Foliage crops*. Ball Publishing, Batavia.

Raupp, M.J., Van Driesche, R.G. and Davidson, J.A. (1993) *Biological Control of Insect and Mite Pests of Woody Landscape Plants: Concepts, Agents and Methods*. University of Maryland, Maryland.

Steiner, M.Y. and Elliott, D.P. (1987) *Biological Pest Management for Interior Plantscapes*, 2nd edn. Alberta Environmental Centre, Vegreville.

Watson, A.K. (ed.) (1993) *Biological Control of Weeds Handbook*. Weed Science Society of America, Champaign.

Yepson, R.B. Jr. (ed.) (1984) *The Encyclopaedia of Natural Insect and Disease Control*. Rodale Press, Emmans.

Some useful World Wide Web sites (several contain hyperlinks to each other as well as further useful sites).

American Phytopathological Society: http://www.apsnet.org/online/archive.asp

Animal & Plant Health Inspection Service; hotlinks to other biological control pages: http://www.aphis.usda.gov/nbci/hotlinks.html

Auburn's Biological Control Institute (BCI), Auburn University: http://www.ag.auburn.edu/bci/bci.html

Biological control at the University of California at Riverside, CA 92 21, USA: http://www.biocontrol.ucr.edu/

Commercial biological control companies: http://www.pestmanagement.co.uk/library/insecthouse/companies/ih036.html

Commercial biological control producers and suppliers World Wide listings: http://www.agrobiologicals.com/index.html

Commercial biological control producer and supplier: http://www.biobest.be

Commercial biological control producer and supplier: http://www.entocare.nl/engels/FrmsetEprodukten.htm

Commercial biological control producer and supplier: http://www.koppert.nl/english/index.html

Commercial biological control producer and supplier: http://www.SyngentaBioline.com

Florida Agricultural Information Retrieval System, University of Florida: http://hammock.ifas.ufl.edu/

Frank Koehler: http//www.koleopterologie.de/gallery (Arbeitsgemeinschaft Rheinischer Koleopterologen)

IPM experts directory: http://www.ipmalmanac.com/experts/index.asu

International Organisation for Biological Control: http://wwwiobc.global

Midwest biological control news: http://www.entomology.wisc.edu/mbcn/land609.html

New York State Agriculture Experimental Station; a guide to the natural enemies of North America: http://www.nysaes.cornell.edu/ent/biocontrol/

North Carolina's National IPM Network by the North Carolina State University: http://ipmwww.ncsu.edu

Ohio Florists Association, USA: http://www.ofa.org

Photographic library, photographs as in this book: http://www.holt-studios.co.uk

Royal Botanic Gardens, Kew, UK: http://www.rbgkew.org.uk/

Royal Horticultural Society, UK: http://www.rhs.org.uk

United States Department of Agriculture: http://www.usda.gov

University of California IPM Home Page, University of California at Davis: http://www.ipm.ucdavis.edu/

University of Nebraska Co-operative Extention: Biological Control of Insect and Mite Pests: http://ianrwww.unl.edu/ianr/pubs/extnpubs/insects/g1251

University of Purdue Co-operative Extension: Purdue's Biological Control Laboratory: http://www.entm.purdue.edu/entomology/bclab/biocontrol.html

Glossary

abdomen – rear part of body of an arthropod
alate – winged
antagonist - enemy
antenna(e) – sensory organ on insect's head, 'feeler'
aposematic – warning (colours)
apterae – wingless
arthropod – animal with external skeleton, jointed legs and segmented body
banker plant system – system where beneficial insects are encouraged onto plants which are then moved to within the main crop to boost biological control numbers
bio-indicator – species used to detect changes
carapace – hard covering of body
cephalothorax – forward section of arachnid body whereby the head and thorax are joined
chaetotaxy – arrangement of bristles on organism's body
cocoon – silky case spun by insect larva for protection of pupa
colonist – species attracted into an area by prey
conidiophore – fungal fruiting body
conidium – fungal spore
crawler – first stage larva of usually sedentary insect
cuticle – waxy layer covering body
damp off – fungal disease of plant roots
detritivore – animal that eats waste
deutonymph – second nymphal stage of mites, after egg and protonymph
diauer larva – infective nematode larva
diapause – hibernation stage induced by low temperatures and shortening day length during autumn, whereby the organism over-winters
dicotyledon – flowering plant that has an embryo with two cotyledons (embryonic leaves)
diurnal – day-active
ecosystem – biological community of interacting organisms and their environment
ectoparasitoid – predator that develops outside the body of prey
elytron(a) – wing case
endoparasitoid – predator that develops within the body of prey
entemopathogenic – causing disease in insects
epidermis – outer layer (of skin, leaf)
epigyne – female spider genital area
epizootic – (disease) widespread throughout a population
filiform – thread-like
fungivore – animal that eats fungi
gall – deformed growth on a plant produced by insects, fungi, mites or nematodes
haltere – club-shaped fly balance organs, modified hindwings
haemolymph – fluid in an insect serving as its blood
hermaphrodite – containing both sets of sexual reproductive organs
honeydew – sugary waste of many phloem-feeding insects
hydroponics – process of growing plants without soil
hyperparasitoid – parasitoid that develops in or on another parasitoid
instar – stage of life between any two moults, adult being the final instar
Integrated Crop Management (ICM) – integration of chemical, biological, cultural and physical control methods to reduce input for sustainable crop production

Integrated Pest Management (IPM) – use of commercially-raised beneficial insects with compatible pesticides
invertebrate – animal lacking backbone
kairomone – scent produced by a host organism that attracts a prey organism
lamina – thin layer (of leaf)
mandible – jaw or mouth-part of an arthropod; it may be toothed for biting or needle-shaped for sucking
maxilla – part of arthropod mouth-part found just behind the jaws, used for handling and sucking chewed food
moult – shedding of outer skin
nocturnal – night-active
nymph – immature form of insect or mite that closely resembles the adult; no pupation occurs to become an adult
ocularium – tubercle bearing a pair of sideways-facing simple eyes
ovipositor – tubular egg-laying organ of insect
palp – segmented sense organ at the mouth of an arthropod
parasitoid – insect that lives in or on another organism for part of its life cycle and eventually kills the host
parthenogenesis – asexual production of young without fertilization of eggs
perennial – plant that lasts through several growing seasons
petiole – ring-like second abdominal segment of a wasp
pheromone – chemical sex attractant used by males
phloem – nutrient conducting tissue of plants
phytophagous – plant eating
pneumostome – pore at rear of slug mantle leading to 'lung'
polyembryony – multiple individuals developing from an egg
polyphagous – eating a variety of organisms
polyvoltine – having several generations each year
proboscis – elongated, sucking mouth-parts of an insect
pronotum – main part of dorsal surface of first thoracic segment
protonymph – first stage after mite egg hatch
pupa – inactive immature stage of an insect in which the larva metamorphoses to the adult
puparium – barrel-shaped case formed from last larval skin in which (mainly fly) pupa is hidden
pyrethroid – naturally occuring pesticides from species of chrysanthemum, usually with short persistence
refugium(a) – area in which a population of organisms can survive during unfavourable conditions
resident - species present throughout growing season
rhizoid – root-like
rostrum – beak-like part of insect or arachnid mouth-parts
senescence – growing old
seta – stiff hair or bristle
spinneret – spinning organ of an arachnid
stylet – piercing mouth-part of an insect and sting of wasp
tarsus(i) – foot or fifth joint of leg of an insect
temperate – of mild climatic conditions
thorax – middle part of the body of an arthropod to which legs and wings (if present) are attached
top fruit – fruit grown on trees
transconjugation – joining of two genetic strains
trichome – sticky hair of plant
under-storey – layer of vegetation under main canopy of trees
univoltine – having only one generation each year
vena spuria – false vein
virion – single virus particle
viviparous – produces live young

Taxonomic Index

Page numbers in **bold** refer to major discussion of organisms in the text

Subject Index